The Crabby Angels No Bullshit Guide
to
Peace, Joy and Prosperity

Brother Jacob Glass

Copyright © 2018 Jacob Glass

All rights reserved.

ISBN: 9781731592255

DEDICATION

In loving memory of the adorable Judy Babcock with eternal gratitude.

Introduction and How to Use This Book

In the summer of 2009, I was living for a year in Palm Springs, California, going through a time of deeper searching and growing again. Palm Springs has always been a very spiritual place for me and those magical purple mountains feed my soul in ways I cannot express. During this time of inner searching, I began to receive guidance from what I see as my "party angels" – Light messengers who continually remind me to "lighten up" and get more joy out of daily living. I started typing out their messages to me on a daily blog which eventually was published as my book, "The Crabby Angels Chronicles" though they are not really crabby at all, just blunt and to-the-point. I cannot begin to tell you of the countless miracles that book brought into my life, how many it deeply touched and helped and the amazing people I have met because of it. I am forever grateful and humbled.

Since then, I published two more Crabby Angel books, "Starve a Bully, Feed a Champion" and "You Were Born for Greatness" which I THOUGHT ended a trilogy and we were done. Well, not so fast because here we are 10 years later and I am still receiving Divine Instruction and reminders every day. Apparently there is more to say and I need constant reminders, so on we go now with book number 4 in a series which may continue on for some time. I am on a continual "need-to-know basis," so I'm not venturing a guess anymore.

Please, know that you can use this book any way you want to because it is now YOUR book. I place it in your hands to make use of in whatever way best serves you.

But please do USE it and make it your own rather than just putting it up on your book shelf to get to one day. This is a book to USE – not just more spiritual information to take in and forget.

Also, you do not have to read the book in order. You can just "plop" it open each day and read whatever page you land on. You could start on the last page and read it from ending to beginning – there really is no order to the lessons. You may read more than one page per day or stay on the same page for a few days. The Angels are FUN and frank and sometimes shocking. Just breathe and enjoy the process. As we lighten up, miracles happen. Thank you for being on this wonderful journey.

Epigraph

"If thou canst believe,

all things are possible to one that believeth.

Mark 9:23

ACKNOWLEDGMENTS

All my amazing miracle worker Stewardship Patrons –
you are rock stars and fabulous AF.

THE LESSONS

1. We Got You Boo

This is the time for faith. You let this goal be set for you. That was an act of faith. Do not abandon faith, now that the rewards of faith are being introduced.

A Course in Miracles

Beloved, let Us walk you through this time of transitions as much as possible. You still take far too much personal responsibility for people and things outside of your circle - not in your yard, basically. This is not helpful to anyone. Let Us handle all the HOW while you focus on the what. Let Us direct all the WHO as well. It's time for you to relax more mentally, but without going unconscious. This is more a joyful relaxation than a sleeping rest. STOP RIGHT NOW and take a deep breath as you let it all go again. STOP. JUST STOP. Release and let go. Exhale out all the bullshit and manipulating and resisting. Let it ALL GO babe.

You are not delegating enough to Us and are energetically TRYING too hard. Let it go. ALLOW Us to take the burden from you. Let Us carry it all as you soothe yourself into alignment. You will see that what then happens will seem more like magic if you get out of the way and release the desire to ACCOMPLISH anything.

Much of your old erroneous thinking has been dissolved in this last leap of learning but there is much more that will need to be dissolved - and most of this has to do with your tendency to be hyper-vigilant in regard to OTHERS. Yes, you are still wound way

Brother Jacob

too tightly over this. But, We have a wonderful gentle plan for gradually undoing all of that if you will again increase your childlike faith and turn over the reins. Remember, We will always lead you to the path of JOY and fun, not down the road of sacrifice and "service" and religious sanctimonious thinking. Keep releasing the hostages - daily, even hourly.

Focus your attention on the JOY. Life is a dance between you and the Universe which is meant to be light and fun. You can afford to relax when you remember this. There is no one to convince, no one you need to sell on this but yourself. Once again We must ask you, how FABULOUS and FUN are you willing to LET your life get this year? How loved, happy, prosperous, healthy, successful and free are you WILLING to be, with no justification or defensiveness? DECIDE, and then turn it over to Us. We're YOUR Team! We got you boo.

2. Don't Push, Align

You who cannot even control yourself should hardly aspire to control the Universe.

A Course in Miracles

If you push hard now, you will find many things breaking rather than yielding and giving way. Pushing is best done very rarely and for very short periods of time. The creation of an entirely new human being has very little effort in it! There is the initial joyous sexual desire and action which may last only minutes, followed by nine months of nothing but nesting. Then, there may be a long labor process and of all that only the very last minutes of that is when the midwife instructs the mother to push. Pushing is usually the very worst way to create or change anything, dear mystic.

Of course, the human world has most things upside down and inside out. People want to go out and "crush it" every day so they can feel justified for being alive and taking up space on the planet. It also gives them the illusion of control. But as you are already well aware, crushing it is a horrible and violent metaphor for the gentle spirit. When you think this way, you are at odds with your Inner Being and are actually far less in alignment with your greater good.

Motivation is exhausting and draining. Inspiration is the way of alignment and harmony with the All. Motivation is about forcing and pushing. Inspiration is like being irresistibly drawn forward from within - like a magnet ATTRACTING YOU TOWARD something. The sexual act of creation is one of inspiration and cosmic desire so even though there is tremendous effort put forth, it does not feel like something you are "motivating" and forcing yourself to do.

THIS is a time for you to LET YOURSELF BE. Keep everything very simple.

Do MORE of what does work.
Do _{less} of what doesn't work.

You are already very aware that whatever you force right now will only bring more frustration and be a very temporary win at best. It's a time to go inside and repair your nets rather than doubling down on your fishing expeditions. You are in a nesting phase and to fight it is to fight nature Herself. Instead of trying to push and force, spend your time ALIGNING with LOVE. Your heart is softening more every day as is typical of the nesting phase. Let it.

As you align with Love, It will draw to you all that you are needing at this time - and all that is truly YOURS, without struggle or forcing, in the same way that the embryo draws nutrients from the atmosphere. Protect your precious dreams now and let them grow slowly in their own timing and ways. Practice radical non-interference and radical alignment with Source. ENJOY this time. Nesting is not doing NOTHING, for any mother can tell you that while there may be a lot of sleeping and resting there is also a lot of outer preparation and even parties. Rooms are decorated, supplies are purchased, there may be knitting and baking and families gathering and all kinds of activities going on. This is where you are now - in a place of joyous gentle preparation.

You will find that many wonderful and seemingly miraculous things will effortlessly walk through the door while you are focusing on preparing rather than forcing. It is not a time of dormancy and deadness, but many things will be happening in the hidden womb before you will feel and see the evidence of them. But if you stay aligned, there will be wonderful manifestations of good all along the way.

And IF you need to push, We'll let you know.

3. Fear Fast/Faith Feast

I am at home. Fear is the stranger here.

A Course in Miracles

It's that time again. Time to clean up your vibration in order to have a much smoother daily ride. It's time to stop tolerating fear, which really is lovelessness. It's time to stop allowing so much passive mind wandering. Yes, it's time for that word DISCIPLINE again.

However, We want you to know that this discipline is not about lack of fun or a severity. It is simply a more diligent retraining of the puppy where you've gotten a little too lax and lazy. We are HELPING YOU already with this. You are NOT alone. You haven't been bad. It's not a punishment. In fact, you might even want to think of it more the way you would about taking your car in to have a "wheel alignment" when it starts "pulling" you off center. We know that you want to have a more effortless driving experience in life - to have a more well-trained and happy puppy.

SO, it's time to turn DOWN the fear and turn UP the faith. Faith is an attribute of Consciousness so it's already THERE, but you have gotten a little out of alignment along the way and put some of that faith in the things of the world, and in works of flesh, instead of ONLY on the Power of God within you. Our goal for you is the happy return to your childlike faith and expectancy of good. Do you agree? Is this what you want? Are you on board?

As far as your puppy mind goes, this is simply a matter of daily diligence in taking your emotional journey and posting that guard at the door of your mind. And in particular, it is about a TOTAL reversal in some areas where you have been putting energy into trying to control other people and conditions and have NOT been controlling YOURSELF. You must do a 180 on this and you will QUICKLY feel tremendous RELIEF and PROGRESS forward. This is very typical human behavior and nothing to feel bad about (just stop doing it) – this habit of making excuses for one's own lack of control while wanting or expecting other people or situations to change according to YOUR standards or desires for them. It's hopeless and a waste of the creative energy that you could be putting into changing YOUR OWN mental habit patterns.

Again, nothing to feel bad about and it can be cleaned up IN AN INSTANT as soon as you turn around and start moving in the right direction again. We are here for you. You CAN do this and once you take the first few steps you will feel momentum growing VERY quickly in the increase of faith in Source and the dissolving of many fears and worries. Shit's about to get very good around here!

4. LET GO AND LAUGH MORE!

Into eternity, where all is one, there crept a tiny, mad idea, at which the Son of God remembered not to laugh. In his forgetting did the thought become a serious idea, possible of both accomplishment and real effects.

A Course in Miracles

Remember that We are the Party Brotherhood. We come eagerly to help you LIGHTEN UP your mind and spirit. *"Getting more out of life"* is all about how light you can let yourself be. Spiritual folks often make the mistake of becoming somber and serious, even depressed and dark from focusing on the pain and suffering in the world, among other mistakes.

Let Us also remind you very clearly that you are NOT your brother's keeper! No one is. Everyone is responsible for self. When Cane guiltily said, *"Am I my brother's keeper?"* he had just MURDERED his brother Abel! He felt guilty because he WAS guilty. Many spiritual humans feel as if they'd killed or robbed someone because of the way religious guilt has warped their minds. You are NOT responsible for anyone but yourself and you ARE helping many others all the time by helping them help themselves. When others are lazy or don't pay attention or aren't listening, that's on them, not you. Learn to laugh it off instead of becoming frustrated or trying to do for them what they are not doing for themselves.

This phase of your learning now will have a lot to do with how much you can and are willing to laugh off the things that once caused you pain and frustration. The more serious you become about your spirituality, the worse everything will get and the more you will suffer and cause suffering. The more light and breezy you are, the more you will attract good into your world and offer good to others. It's really quite simple, but it is definitely a principle of Opposite World and not of the culture around you. Stay strong in your joy brother - We have much to offer you in this year of increasing ease and fun. Your Light will attract others who are ready to drop their burdens and join the party!

5. Isn't It Wonderful?

Notice how God is is-ing every single minute as leaves, flowers and fruit. And the miracle is that nobody is praying for it; nobody is asking for it; nobody is telling God how much he needs these things - the fruit and vegetables and cattle on a thousand hills. And yet in spite of that, God is attending to all of it.

Joel Goldsmith

One of your songs tells you that *"love is all you need"* and you are already very aware of how problematic that word "love" is to the human race - so, We'd like to assist you by slightly changing that up to say *"ALIGNMENT is all you need."* When you are in alignment with Source, all is well with you even if the circumstances are not to your liking. Alignment with Source is not dependent on whether there is another person around or not, or whether you are physically feeling well or not, whether there are funds in the bank or not, whether your dreams are coming true or even if not one thing seems to be going according to your plans. Alignment is an awareness of Oneness with Source. And this removes all need to pray for anything to change or be taken care of by God. Source is already sourcing everything fully. YOUR job is to align with that rather than trying to get some deity to align with YOU. Everything is ALREADY well. And if you can RELAX even in the middle of seeming crisis, you will find your alignment and therefore find your peace and Answer.

All Treatment work is about this - alignment. It does nothing to God, nothing to the Universe, nothing to anyone or anything outside of you. Your Treatments and affirmations are TOOLS OF

ALIGNMENT, and when YOU are in alignment, then the things outside of you have PERMISSION to change if change would be beneficial. All your resistance and trying to FORCE things is what KEEPS them stuck the way they are through the power of your attention and activation. But as you know these are only two of many many tools to return you to alignment. It's highly individual. You may also find yourself aligned by nature, music, dancing, walking the dog, napping, petting the cat, sucking the dick, laughing at the comedian, cooking, working on the car . . . you get the idea. The more you can relax your mind, the more you will find yourself effortlessly slipping into alignment and smoothly gliding along the highlighted route again. Isn't it wonderful? How wonderful to not have to tell God how to be God, to not have to instruct the Universe on how to turn a seed into a flower or how to make the planets revolve around the sun.

And it is exponentially more fabulous when you realize it is nothing you need to EARN. There are so many erroneous concepts on your planet about earning money, earning love, earning respect, earning time off and so on. What many humans do not realize is that they must RELAX their way into alignment. You cannot work yourself into alignment. Of course the relaxing is of the MIND and spirit. Your body may be rock climbing or conducting a symphony or running a marathon as you relax your way into alignment. You can actually PLAY your way into the life of your dreams if your dreams are not rigidly attached to some outer picture of things. As you relax and play your way into alignment the Universe will effortlessly and elegantly deliver the ESSENCE of everything that you have ever wanted or desired. ESSENCE, not necessarily form. Relax. All is well. Isn't that wonderful to know?

And We feel you slipping more into alignment every day now as you spend time with Us each morning again. We are very happily busy "greasing your wheels" for a smoother and smoother ride. And notice how hard it ISN'T. Answering the Call is not hard at all - it's resisting the Call that wears people down.

You're welcome.

6. Try Softer

You can know if you've succeeded in prayer by how you feel. If you remain worried or anxious, and if you are wondering how, when, where, or through what source your answer will come, you are meddling . . . remind yourself that Infinite Intelligence is taking care of the problem in Divine Order, and far better than you could do by the tense efforts of your conscious mind.

Joseph Murphy

When you keep opening the oven to see if the bread is baking, you are letting out the heat and are in fact slowing down the process by which bread bakes. Once you've done your part, sit back and relax. Your part is to have the happy desire and to live in the Consciousness of it already having been accomplished - not to micromanage every step. FAITH is the ability to relax and trust the Flow to flow.

More than anything right now, We want you to focus on your own bread and not on how other people are or are not baking their bread. The tendency among humans to get involved in "helping" others has caused more problems than it has brought solutions. Save yourself and others are inspired to save themselves. Think of all the horrors of those Christians who violently went about trying to "save" the "pagan savages" over the centuries. It is not much different today. Meddling is one of the main problems of humankind - on a global scale and on a personal family and workplace scale.

So many times you have thought that you were "warning" others about this or that and found that all it did was upset YOU and they did exactly what they were going to do anyhow. Except now you'd gotten yourself all worked up, ruined your peace and joy, and all for nothing. Even when people ASK for help there is an excellent chance that they will not accept or receive it!

YOUR job is to remain non-attached while you BLESS THEM, give them the information and then pay not the least bit of attention to whether they use it or not. You must bless them and trust that they have their own Guidance and you are not here to take over as guide for another. Let God be God. Offer and give what you are comfortable giving without strings and then let them work out their own salvation.

As the Tao says, if you are a truly effective teacher and leader, whether as a mother or grandfather or personal trainer or artist, or business owner or anything else, the people will say, *"We did it ourselves!"* And you will be thrilled by that because you will be busy in our own kitchen having delicious bread just out of the oven. Trust the process. Your joy will do more to heal others than 1,000 crusades could ever do. Stop trying so HARD. Try softer while you relax and breathe, relax and breathe. All is well if you are not judging according to appearances.

7. THERE IS NO SECRET

Simplicity is very difficult for twisted minds.

A Course in Miracles

As you well know by now, there is no one out there with secret esoteric knowledge that you do not have. That is a marketing ploy by "spiritual teachers" who know that humans BELIEVE that there is something missing in them so they take advantage of that belief. The Truth is simple and basic and unglamorous in a world in which people want endless variety and entertainment. Stick to the simple path and let everyone else go their own way.

This is true of most everything. Simple eating and simple exercise work and yet the humans are endlessly touting some latest "it" that will be SO DIFFERENT and NEW. And it's not. There is nothing new under the sun, only new advertising and hype. And sales are almost exclusively based on first creating self-doubt and fear in the "customer" and then filling the false need. Life hacks and Ted talks and super soul Sundays and weekend workshops are all harmless enough if you realize that they are just maps - they are not the territory and they are NOT the GPS. They are still tools of the limited mind and they all have advertisers and sponsors who want to get something from you.

YOU are whole already. There is nothing missing and no one has the "top" spiritual information to give to you - they're just repackaging the same old, same old. Walk the plain simple path and your world will be lit by miracles rather than by neon billboards. Let everyone go chasing after the trendy new this or that while you keep your blinders on doing your own thing. Stick with one thing that works and let the rest go even while the whole world is running after the shiny new thing. Listen to what is simple. Read what is simple and don't look for what is NEXT. As long as you keep on doing what works, you'll keep on having good results. When you stop doing it, the results will go away. It is extremely simple and your culture DESPISES simplicity.

Your way is very different because it is part of Opposite World. You will thrive by attraction, not promotion. In Opposite World you are magnetic and don't need to change to fit the current culture trends. *"Stand ye still and see the salvation of the Lord"* means that you can call off the search for anything and everything. Stand on Principle, resting in the Presence and your good will come running to you like a puppy rolling in ecstasy at your feet. Life is meant to be simple, joyous and fun. Stop complicating it with your thinking. LET Life love you today without your effort and struggle. You're perfect already.

8. CANCEL YOUR FUTURE

If you want stress on purpose, get a future.

Byron Katie

You do have a tendency to get way out ahead of yourself at times - and this is one of those times. And all that means is that it is the ideal time for you to return to the gentle faith of a child and the practice of *"just do one thing, just do one thing, just do one thing"* that Byron Katie taught you. You are sneakily trying to figure out what is going to happen and HOW. We are going to remind you to stop this quite frequently for, oh let's say the next 20 years or so, on a daily and perhaps hourly basis. Please don't let it annoy you. We will not leave you to your own thinking without constant Guidance on Our end. YOU can delete your past and cancel your future by placing them both in the hands of God so that you can live in a most joyous NOW. In Reality, there is no such thing as a past or future, there is only the never ending now, now, now.

And yes, it is the perfect time for you to fast from fear while feasting on large mouthfuls of faith, faith and more faith. We've got your file right here in front of us 24/7 and have not fallen asleep on the job. Please stop 2nd guessing Us and Our methods - and stop doubting yourself. Stop judging according to appearances - they are ever-changing and unstable. Turn within and find your stability there with Us.

In fact, more than ever in your journey this time around We want you to go SILENT as much as possible in order to go within. Turn AWAY from the meaningless distractions of the outer world as much as possible and strengthen your spirit by hanging on the Vine within. This will take tremendous diligence and determination on your part for you have gotten into the habit of observing people you barely know across the internet for many more hours than you spend connecting to Source and your own Inner Being. It's time to reverse that now and We will Help you with that too. Again, THIS is the ideal time for all of this because it is a time of being truly FED by spiritual meat for adults rather than the milk for babies. We ARE preparing you to bear greater fruit in the coming season than you have ever born before, but first You must allow us to prune back all that is not bearing good fruit. Relax and let everything that goes, go. Cling to nothing, regret nothing, mourn none of it. It is a joyous preparation for the Spring which is about to come!

9. SOURCE IS YOUR SOURCE OF COURSE OF COURSE

Whatever is of God is Self-maintained and Self-sustained. If you realize that, you will not lose faith and you will not be afraid of losing . . . You will not fear competition.

— Joel Goldsmith

You live in a world of "hype" and bullshit. Perhaps no time in human history has been more reflective of the story of "The Emperor Has No Clothes" than the one you live in now. And you must remain very very vigilant for Truth instead of letting yourself fall under the hypnotism of the bullshit again. The answers and Ted talks and life hacks and such that the human culture offer you are just more of the rearranging of the deck chairs on the Titanic. That sucker is going DOWN while the culture has you running around doing meaningless busy work.

Nothing real and nothing that is truly yours can ever be lost. Loss and gain are only of the physical, but the content is what you REALLY want anyhow. You must not be like Lot's wife forever looking behind you until you solidify and are frozen. Focus on what you HAVE, not on what you HAD if you want the peace and joy of God. There is nothing back there in the past for you anymore. All your power and good is in the present moment.

Yes, bodies come and go, money goes up and down, houses are bought and sold and the world goes round and round. But YOU are stable and sure-footed if you keep your eyes on the Kingdom and NOT on the insane world of the culture. You can not be happy while being mesmerized by the culture "out there." Come inside as frequently as possible during the day, even for seconds at a time.

Remember that YOU are a Divine creation and are therefore Divinely maintained and sustained. The same is true of your life when you remember your Source is nothing of the culture. Remember your True Source at any given moment and you cannot help but remember that you are safe and all is well. There is no lack, no scarcity, no competition, no limit to your resources. When you tune-in to your Source, you show up on the Radar as a big fucking BLIP BLIP BLIP which makes it easier and easier for your good to find YOU. You can call off all searching. So relax baby. Relax your way into alignment again every time you feel "off." In your creation work, focus on creating a FEELING more than any condition and then let the FEELING be the thing that brings the conditions that match it. Much easier and more efficient. And the better you feel, the better you feel.

10. FUCK FAIRNESS

All special relationships have sin as their goal. For they are bargains with reality, toward which the seeming union is adjusted. Forget not this - to bargain is to set a limit, and any brother with whom you have a limited relationship <u>you</u> hate. You may attempt to keep the bargain in the name of "fairness," sometimes demanding payment of yourself, perhaps more often of the other. Thus in the "fairness" you attempt to ease the guilt that comes from the accepted purpose of the relationship. And that is why the Holy Spirit must change its purpose to make it useful to <u>him</u> and harmless unto <u>you</u>.

- A Course in Miracles

You may remember that the Course tells you that God's laws are always fair. Always. But humans are not. Organizations are not. Groups and anything of your world is not. In the human sense, fairness is just another concept that fills you with rage and depression when you find some evidence of "unfairness" in your life or world. Let it go. If you want the peace of God, then you must release the world from such concepts and once again remember your Source.

Your Source is totally fair, always. When you place a demand on the Law, that is correct. When you place that demand on people, places and conditions, you seek suffering and disappointment. Fuck fairness in your human interactions. Instead, simply be sure that YOU are always coming from a place of honesty, integrity, not trying to take advantage of or manipulating anyone, not being shady or a hustler. That is ALL. YOUR end is what you have control over. And the seeds YOU sow will bear fruit, but not necessarily from that person, that business or romantic relationship, or that situation. They are not your source.

Remember, you are not asking a human or organization to be fair or to give you what you want - they are only an avenue. You are actually making the demand of your Source, the limitless expansive Universe. Therefore, you can go BIG in your demands. You don't have to trust people because you can trust your Source. Humans are mostly terrified, this makes them very unstable. ONLY your Source is stable. Source is fair. Source is honest. Source is dependable. Source is unfailing. Neither do you need to seek for retribution against "wrongdoers" for everyone reaps what they sow in good time.

Whatever you may have "lost" to an "unfair" or dishonest person or situation can be restored "double for your trouble" if you will call on the Law of Divine Compensation rather than in continuing to attack and defend against the human world. As long as you hold your grievance, the Law cannot work for you and you under the laws of man rather than the laws of God. Under the laws of man, the one with the best lawyer or manipulation skills "wins." Then you will harm yourself by building up bigger and bigger "defenses" to "protect" yourself from future loss. But all you do is create an attract more clever liars and thieves. You create what you defend against.

Let it all go and return to the Spiritual Truth rather than the limited fallible human "truth." Let Us handle the TRUE fairness of everything while you continue to ask of yourself, "What joyful thing do I want to create out of this?"

11. Fuck the World

This course does not attempt to take from you the little that you have. It does not try to replace utopian ideas for satisfactions which the world contains . . . There is no world!
— A Course in Miracles

"The world" is just a concept. Frequently it is a concept which overwhelms, disturbs and upsets you because you are seeing it through the heavy filter that is shown to you through flickering images on screens. But no two people see or live in the same world. Fuck the concept of a "world." The Answer to any problem of "a world" is very simple and is all that anything is ever about anyhow . . . Are you ready?

Just love the "asshole" in front of you right now.

We're not talking about liking or approving of them. We're not talking about "affection" or ooey gooey feelings. We're talking about viewing them without attack or condemnation. Once again, the Answer is to "go soft" instead of hard. See people with gentleness, and YOUR concept of the world will begin to shift immediately.

YOU are creating YOUR concept of a world with every thought that you think. If the world you see terrifies or disturbs you, it is because of your own perception. "The world" changes in your mind before you SEE the change "out there." Perception CAUSES seeing. You may not even realize that you have DECIDED what you will see in the world, because the decision is made at an unconscious level. And you CAN change your mind - first consciously, and then through repetition, that choice will be impressed upon your subconscious mind.

DECIDE. CHOOSE. What "world" do you WANT to see? Here are some options:

I see a world of gentleness and beauty.
I see a world of love and kindness.
I see a world of wealth and possibilities for me.
I see a world that works for most.
I see a world of health and vitality for me.
I see a world of friendship and harmony.
I see a world of joy and happiness for me.
I see a world of limitless opportunities for me.
I see a world lit by miracles and grace.
I see a world in which it is safe for me to love and be loved.

12. IT'S OKAY, IT'S OKAY, IT'S OKAY

Prepare you now for the undoing of what never was. If you already understood the difference between truth and illusion, the Atonement would have no meaning . . . Put yourself not in charge of this, for you cannot distinguish between advance and retreat. Some of your greatest advances you have judged as failures, and some of your deepest retreats you have evaluated as success.

- A Course in Miracles

You really must stop judging your path according to appearances. You too often think in terms of form rather than content. The content is the FEELING, the ESSENCE. Your beauty has nothing to do with the illusion seen in a mirror. Your abundance and wealth cannot be seen on a bank statement. Your worthiness cannot be evaluated by how much you have checked off your "to do" list or by how many people you think you have helped that day. And when you are afraid it is always because you have once again let ego steal your joy and are judging according to appearances of loss, limitation and separation. Stop it. Let it go. Breathe. There is no enemy - nothing to be conquered or defeated.

You are NOT going to be okay. You already ARE okay, right now. This is not about later. We are RIGHT here and you are not alone. Even now, all things are held perfectly in the hands of God. You have no idea how huge your Team is! There are those you knew in the physical who have come back to the non-physical who are cheering you on and often protecting you (from yourself) as much as possible while not interfering with your free will or desires. Additionally, We are always with you and are not only available at your slightest invitation, but We NEVER judge you in the least.

Worry is nothing more than an affirming that you are not okay, that it is not okay. If We were capable of being insulted, We would take offense. Oh ye of little faith! We are never on a coffee break or out running an errand. We never find you demanding or "needy." It is Our great pleasure to Help as much as you are willing to be helped. But there is no need to whine or plead your case. Ask and it is given - just don't fucking micromanage Us. We see things you cannot possibly see. We see the BIG picture and the road ahead. We know easily and immediately what you only know deep deep within yourself. We know the best paths and timing. Relax. Relax. Relax. And KNOW that it IS okay. Have some confidence and faith. Fear not. Be not afraid. Good shit is on the way, but you have to be relaxed enough to let it get through. YOUR work is about enjoying the journey.

13. YOUR VALUE

Your worth is not established by teaching or learning. Your worth is established by God. Nothing you think or wish or make is necessary to establish your worth.

- A Course in Miracles

In many ways, this is the foundation of this entire teaching We have come to impart. You are not a sinner, not broken, not a disappointment. <u>You already ARE worthy and your limitless value has been set by the Source</u>. And just as nothing you do increases your value, nothing you have done or could do will ever diminish it. There is no punishing God anywhere but in the mythology of the ego.

Your true value and worth has already been set - but the question is, what value have YOU set on yourself? As you must know, the world you see outside of you is merely a reflection of your own beliefs and concepts. Therefore, you will seem to be valued by others in accordance with the value YOU set on yourself. You must take yourself out of the sale bin and stop marking yourself down. You are top shelf stuff! But YOU must know that about yourself.

What are you saying TO yourself ABOUT yourself? This is more important than anything that anyone else will ever say to you. Yes, when you were a small child you may have been brainwashed by others into thinking negative things about yourself, but YOU can reverse those mental patterns little by little with patience and persistence.

Speak to yourself with love and kindness, patience and encouragement. Set your value HIGH and keep steadily raising it as you go - not in comparison with anyone else, but simply as your own unique self. You are no better or worse than anyone who lives or has ever lived. Stop all comparing and competition with anyone, including with any ridiculous comparison to your younger self or to some fantasy ideal about yourself in your mind. <u>RIGHT NOW, you are fabulous wonderful and a delight to the entire Cosmos</u>. Get on board with that and stop arguing against it. Stop gathering up evidence from the past about how you are a fuckup. JUST STOP.

Take that same fact-finding talent and this time use it to gather up evidence that you are a lovable wonderful child of the Universe. Then, see others that way too. We will be repeating this lesson over and over in various ways in the coming days so that you do not replace it with fear thoughts and self attack. Treat yourself as the valuable treasure that you ARE.

What are 3 things that you love or appreciate about yourself right now?

14. GIVING AND GETTING

The cost of giving is receiving . . . Who understands what giving means must laugh at the idea of sacrifice . . . To give and receive are one in truth.

- A Course in Miracles

You could just as easily and truthfully say that the cost of inhaling is exhaling. There is no more bullshit theory among the humans than that of "selflessness" and sacrificial service and giving. It was a concept created by the ego's religions to control the masses of people through guilt and shame. It is utterly meaningless and without value because it defies the logic of the Infinite Universe.

It is WISE and right to give in order to receive. It is HOW all of Life is set up. FIRST is the giving or sowing, followed by the getting or reaping. Nothing could be more simple and straightforward. But of course simplicity is very difficult for twisted tormented minds which prefer to MAKE everything as complicated and fucked up as possible with the most unnecessary steps added.

Return to simplicity dear Mystic. See this Principle everywhere. If you want to get a baby, sperm must be first given. THAT is how simple and basic to LIFE this Principle is. You are told to go out and be FRUITFUL and the only way to do that is to engage in the process of GETTING FRUIT. There is nothing "selfless" about it and no reason to feel guilty. The Source has commanded BE FRUITFUL - GET FRUIT GOING! Your PURPOSE is to be FRUITFUL.

You must stop being "spiritual" about this and get REAL. But remember, it is not a direct line back and forth when it comes to the giving in relationships, whether personal or business. In other words, you may give and sow in one relationship, but reap in a totally different one. Don't get attached to the physical - focus on the ENERGY FLOWING and don't decide where or who it must flow from.

Start to get used to the idea of getting what you want and getting more out of Life. And prime the pump by giving more, with more INTENTION. INTEND to be fruitful from your giving.

15. BE A SNOB

The purpose of the Atonement is to restore everything to you, or rather to restore it to your awareness. You were given everything when you were created, just as everyone was. When you have been restored to the recognition of your original state, you naturally become part of the Atonement yourself. <u>As you share my inability to tolerate lack of love in yourself and others</u>, you must join the Great Crusade to correct it. The slogan for the Crusade is "Listen, learn and <u>do</u>": Listen to my voice, learn to undo error, and <u>do</u> something to correct it.

- A Course in Miracles

We really want you to become "vibrational snobs" when it comes to how picky you should be about what you are doing with your energy and the energies you are exposing yourself to on a regular basis. This has nothing to do with "better or worse" so much as it has to do with clear or scattered, high or low frequencies, valuable and valueless, fruitful or not. You need to PAY ATTENTION to the ENERGIES in words, and situations, and places, then CHOOSE carefully. You cannot afford to be mindless anymore.

Just as you would not go to a buffet and just take one of everything whether you like or not just because it is there, you should not do this with your vibration and just pick up all the flotsam and jetsam of the world around you simply because it is available or out of not wanting to "upset" anyone by not coming to their event, etc. We are asking you to be COURAGEOUS and STRONG about this and to be FIRM with yourself. You should not tolerate mind wandering and vibration lowering within yourself. Be kind, but firm. What do you THINK you deserve? That is what you will allow.

Be at least as picky about your vibration as you are about what you order in a restaurant. Don't go places where you are dishonored or where the vibration is about dishonoring others. Don't lower your Consciousness in order to "relate" to others. You are NOT doing them a favor AT ALL.

And you don't have to make a big deal out of it or be dramatic or make pronouncements to anyone. Simply be willing at any moment to pick up your keys and walk out and head to Higher Ground when possible. Be willing to change the subject to something of a higher frequency. This is the willingness to DO. And if it is not possible at the time, remember to surround yourself in the God Bubble which will filter out all lower frequencies and allow in and out only the Christ Light. Be picky about this. Be a vibrational snob.

16. THE RISE OF MIRACLES AND MAGIC

Miracles are natural. When they do <u>not</u> occur, something has gone wrong . . . Miracles are everyone's right, but purification is necessary first . . . You are a miracle, capable of creating in the likeness of your Creator. Everything else is only your own nightmare and does not exist. Only the creations of light are real.
- A Course in Miracles

It's time. You ARE ready. The days of NEEDING a miracle must end now so that you can live in a state where they are the NORM for you. It is time to let go of NEEDING to be saved from this or that and using a miracle once in a blue moon to get you through some difficulty that most likely you got yourself into to begin with. The Infinite Sunlit age of miracles and magic is rising for you now beloved.

Again, you are a CREATOR not a reactor. You did not come forth to simply react to the shitstorm of the egoic world of war and low consciousness. You came forth to CREATE from out of NOTHING your OWN world and Reality. You have allowed that thought system to teach you that there is some value in being "down to earth" when nothing could be WORSE for you. You are made of stardust, not dirt. Stop wallowing in the mud and get your head up in the clouds reaching for the stars as is your Divine Destiny!

Too often, you have let yourself be talked out of the knowledge of Who and What you really are. You have been afraid of seeming irresponsible, or strange or looking weird, but in the ego world the BEST thing you can be is weird and different from that fucked up "norm." TODAY is the appointed time for you to claim your Divine Inheritance and to RISE UP from the hypnosis of the ego thought system. We are her with you, as ever. We will Help you as much as you allow and want. EXPECT MIRACLES AND MAGIC today. Then, do it again tomorrow. And the next day. and the next. And so on.

17. Insist on Miracles

You can do anything I ask. I have asked you to perform miracles, and have made it clear that miracles are natural, corrective, healing and universal. There is nothing they cannot do, but they cannot be performed in the spirit of doubt or fear. When you are afraid of anything, you are acknowledging its power to hurt you. Remember that where your heart is, there is your treasure also. You believe in what you value. If you are afraid, you are valuing wrongly.

- A Course in Miracles

You must search vigilantly for any scraps of hoping and wishing that you have associated with miracles and ROOT THEM OUT for they will inhibit your demonstrations and delay your miracles. Wishing and hoping are manifestations of DOUBT. Doubt and fear are vicious siblings, bringing confusion and timidity where there should be CONVICTION and DETERMINATION!

Remember that miracles do not really transcend the physical laws - they demonstrate that you do not KNOW what the ACTUAL Laws are. This is why a major aspect of miracles is that they UNDO rather than DO. YOU must be willing to "come undone" in a sense. This is the undoing of your erroneous beliefs and limiting thoughts.

Miracles are not an unusual fluke which comes along to "save" you or anyone else. They are meant to be as mundane and ordinary as your next breath coming. BUT YOU MUST BECOME MIRACLE-MINDED in order to invoke and recognize them.

When you hear stories of a mother lifting a car off her child trapped beneath, that is a puny demonstration of what miracles are capable of accomplishing. The true miracle is the recognition that the mother had that power within her ALL along but has not been activating or using it except in "dire emergencies." THIS IS THE ERROR. Miracles are corrective, but more on the level of thought, awareness and belief SO that YOU can manifest in limitless ways on a daily, hourly, moment-by-moment basis. But too many "metamagicians" only think to use the Power for parking places and to notice 11:11 on the clock. WTF? Miracles are not parlor tricks.

It's time for you to begin INSISTING on miracles rather than hoping for them. Hoping means you still think they are somehow coming from the outside of you. THERE IS NOTHING OUTSIDE OF YOU. You must stop FEARING YOUR OWN DIVINE POWER AND REALITY. It's time to start having FUN with all of this. JOY is the greatest accelerant to your miracle faculties.

Don't get nervous about this. YOU do not have to decide WHAT the miracle will be or HOW it will happen. That is not your part. Leave that to the Law to work out FOR you. YOUR part is to awaken every day knowing yourself to be a miracle worker with a Divine Power animating and running through you. You part is to devote each day to miracles by invoking them and throwing away all wishing and hoping. Say to the Divinity within you:

> *Here I am! Show me Your love and joyfully use me to manifest miracles on the earth today. Heal my mind and speak to me, guiding me to where You would have me go, doing what You would have me do, and speaking to whom You would have me speak. And let's make it fucking FUN! I'm expecting diamond clusters of miracles all day today and am excited to see how it all continues to unfold.*

Crabby Angels NO BULLSHIT Guide to Peace, Joy and Prosperity

18. Call Off the Search - Again!

Seek not outside yourself. For it will fail, and you will weep each time an idol falls. Heaven cannot be found where it is not, and there can be no peace excepting there. Each idol that you worship when God calls will never answer in His place. There is no other answer you can substitute and find the happiness His answer brings. Seek not outside yourself. For all your pain comes simply from a futile search for what you want, insisting where it must be found. What if it is not there? Do you prefer that you be right or happy? Be you glad that you are told where happiness abides and seek no longer elsewhere. You will fail. But it is given you to know the truth and not to seek for it outside yourself.

- A Course in Miracles

This is another one of those lessons that We like to repeat regularly in order to alleviate your suffering and increase your inner peace and joy. Remember that the dictate of the ego thought system is *"seek but do not find."* And this is the great suffering of the human world. The humans have been suffering and striving since Cane killed Abel over simple jealousy and not getting his way. Your way is quite different for you are a CREATOR!

Remember that Dorothy ran all over the illusory world of Oz trying to find "home," thinking she had to steal a witch's broom and jump through a million hoops, seeking outside of herself every step of the way, living in victim consciousness, and like so many, renouncing her own Power to consult yet another phony spiritual teacher calling himself "great" who was simply a quivering bumbling man hidden behind a curtain!

Finally, after needlessly running herself to exhaustion, even stealing and killing, and watching everyone get what they want EXCEPT her, she is beaten enough to let the fuck go and give up the search! And only THEN can the Christ show up as the Good Witch to let her know that she was 1,000 times more powerful than any wizard outside of her and that only SHE could make her own dreams come true.

STOP chasing after the witches and wizards in all their millions of forms and simply PLAY with your friends. Let your JOY carry you from place to place to place from now on. JOY is miracle fuel. JOY awakens the Wizard in YOU. Skipping down the yellow brick road only becomes frightening when you think you have some serious thing you have to make happen. Then YOU create all kinds of obstacles and flying monkeys to start a war with. Call it off! Get back to your JOY. Get busy playing. Let your good FIND YOU by being the bright Light you ARE. Then, watch the magic happen.

19. Revision Creates Repeal

Miracles are both beginnings and endings. They thus alter the temporal order. They are always affirmations of rebirth which seem to go back but really go forward. They <u>undo the past in the present</u> and thus release the future . . .

The miracle, as an expression of true human charity, can only shorten time at most. It must be understood, however, that whenever one offers a miracle to another, she is shortening the suffering of both. This introduces a correction into the whole record which corrects <u>retroactively</u> as well as progressively.

- A Course in Miracles

How many times have you relived a disturbing past experience, and FELT the upset of it all over again, and perhaps even ADDED to or exaggerated the experience? Too many to count. So it's not as if We are asking you to do something that is at all unusual in asking you to review disturbing episodes of the past - it's simply that We want you to take Us with you so you can revise and rewrite them in ways that are miraculous rather than fearful.

They do not even need to be the ACTUAL incidents, particularly if you find them extremely upsetting. You can write a new scene in which that never happened at all - particularly since reality is always in your own mind anyhow. It's ALL happening in your mind through your perception, until you begin SEEING with the Spiritual Eye and are seeing only love, love, love. For instance, if someone close to you passed over into the non-physical in a particularly disturbing way, you can imagine them passing very quietly and peacefully in their sleep surrounded by loved ones. Or, if you slipped and hurt yourself and are very sore, you can imagine that you caught yourself in time or never slipped at all. Actually, this is an act of forgiveness.

After all, forgiveness is a "selective remembering " in which you remember ONLY the love given and the love received. For this you need the Help of the Holy Spirit (otherwise known as the Spiritual Eye). Make this a regular habit in your Miracles Tool Kit. You may wish to do it right now with Us. Reflect on anything in the past day or week which you found unpleasant or disturbing whether it involved other people or only yourself. Sit quietly and together let us revise it like a playwright at a dress rehearsal with the actor, rewriting a scene that isn't quite working. Keep rewriting it and working with it until it FEELS GOOD to you.

Then, once it's set, release it and go on with your day, feeling as you would feel had the incident played out according to your new updated script. Then, watch the miracles happen. You ARE creating your own reality. Have FUN with it!

20. A World That Works for Everyone

Projection makes perception. The world you see is what you gave it, nothing more than that. But though it is not more than that, it is not less. Therefore, to you it is important. It is the witness to your state of mind, the outside picture of an inward condition. As a man thinketh, so does he perceive. Therefore, seek not to change the world, but will to change your mind about the world. Perception is a result, not a cause. And that is why order of difficulty in miracles is meaningless. Everything looked upon with vision is healed and holy. Nothing perceived without it means anything. And where's there is no meaning, there is chaos.

— A Course in Miracles

A world that works for everyone is already here and always has been. Yearning for a world that works for everyone is much like wanting "a gravity that works for everyone." It's already HERE NOW. In a Universe that is law-based, the laws work for everyone the same. Gravity knows no "privileged" class of people. Law is no respecter of persons. Rich people and poor people fall to the ground if they step off the roof of a building. The Universal laws of attraction and creation are the same.

EVERYONE is attracting and seeing what they are believing, whether seeming slave or king. Period. Gravity works the same for everyone, and your world works the same for everyone. It is a screen on which you project YOUR movie. True, not everyone manifests the same reality, but that is due to belief, not the favor of Source or luck or privilege. Tens of thousands of "privileged class" people die of drug addiction, suicide and alcoholism every year. They are enslaved by a THOUGHT SYSTEM, not an economic system.

True Creators are not seeking a feathered nest to do their manifesting FOR them. You came to this realm WANTING to build your own nest YOUR way but, you quickly forgot that under the hypnotic spell of the culture. NOW is your time of remembering the Truth about Who you are and what is possible for YOU. But YOU must do the daily work of CHOOSING. There is no room for wishy-washy Creators if you want to live in the JOY of the Kingdom. Wishing and hoping ain't gonna do it, baby. Praying and petitioning to a mythical dude in the sky ain't gonna help one bit. Only God-in-YOU can do what needs doing to manifest the world YOU want to see.

It's all about alignment, alignment, alignment - and believing, believing, believing - and feeling, feeling, feeling. All of this leads to seeing, seeing, seeing. This means gathering up the evidence FOR the world YOU WANT, instead of evidence for the world the culture wants you to believe in.

SO, what JOYFUL focus can you have today? How can you make YOUR heart sing today? That is up to YOU. It may come from treating yourself to something, petting the cat, singing and dancing, helping someone else, giving a present, working in the garden, or any limitless number of things. YOUR world changes only when YOU change your MIND about it. Think of it as fearful, and it will be a horror show. Think of it as friendly, prosperous, supportive and loving, and you are in a garden paradise. Your choice. Choose carefully and deliberately. AND you can always change your mind.

21. DEATH IS BULLSHIT

We call it death, but it is liberty. It does not come in forms that seem to be thrust down in pain upon unwilling flesh, but as a gentle welcome to release. If there has been true healing, this can be the form in which death comes when it is time to rest a while from labor gladly done and gladly ended. Now we go in peace to freer air and gentler climate, where it is not hard to see the gifts we gave were saved for us. For Christ is clearer now; His vision more sustained in us; His Voice, the Word of God, more certainly our own.

- A Course in Miracles

There can be no end to true Life. You are you wherever "you" go. Discarding the body does not suddenly render you something else, for you were never that body to begin with. Are you still "you" when you take off a sweater? The body is nothing more than an organic suit of clothes to wear so that others can "see" you in your denser physical environment. You have always been YOU. Therefore, you would do very well to stop all resistance against yourself. You will never be able to "get rid of" yourself.

And by the same token, you have never "lost" anyone simply because they have dropped the body. They are still who they were, only lighter, freer and without any of the impediments or aging of the physical. That brain which had mental illness no longer exists - so all thought is true clear thought. There are no "missing" limbs or "faulty" parts anymore. Those petty resentments, grievances, jealousy, phobias and fears? Gone, gone, gone.
Communication is not only still possible but it is much easier because it is possible any place at any time. There is no need for close physical proximity of bodies, or for technology to bridge the gap of distance. There is no longer the worry of being

misunderstood or interpreted wrongly, for words are not the real means of communication any longer.

Most humans experience physical incarnation like a long "event" for which they've put on a very tight foundation garment in order to "look good" to other bodies. Then what you call death is experienced as coming home after this long event, taking off the tight under garment, kicking off those uncomfortable shoes and plopping down on the sofa for a foot rub from a loved one. Does that sound scary and like something to be dreaded? The "form" it comes in is meaningless - even if the body was "murdered" or the change came in some way you find disturbing or unacceptable. It is still laid down gently by the Spirit within. And NO ONE dies alone. Your Guide is always, always, always with you the moment you call, but particularly at the moment of transition you are tended to on both sides of the journey without distance.

Your loved ones who have made this transition are always so happy to hear from you because they are no longer distracted by their old tight garment. They are relaxed on the cosmic sofa and open and able to hear and SEE you in a way that was not always possible when they were at "the event" with you. They have not left or abandoned you at the party - they've merely gone into another room separated by a thin transparent curtain. THAT is how close your true home is and your "deceased" loved ones are. It is SO not a big deal at all. In Reality, there is no death at all, only yet another change. Everyone is safe, it's only change.

22. Grace is a Presence

Now it was evident that my failure was in believing that I had the power to succeed or fail, when all I could ever be was an instrument for the power of the Divine. God alone is the principle of life. The only success that can come in this world is God's success.

- Joel Goldsmith, Living by Grace

Leave the world of "powers" behind you dear miracle worker. Rest your weary mind as you release "mind power" and "heart power" so that you can know that you have no need of power at all. Only the truly weak think in terms of power - even the "power of love." Love and grace are not powers. Stop seeking for powers and fixes. Instead, rest in the PRESENCE of love and grace. Grace is a presence. True love, not egoic attachment to bodies, is a presence.

God-in-you IS the real you, and you can lean on that more than on any mind power or heart power. The Divine has NO opposite to be a power over. Illness, poverty, separation, pain and loss are all temporary mirages that need not be battled - therefore what need do you have for any power? There is not even any need to surrender, for there is no war. Just let go.

Give up your ideas of loss and gain, failure and success, good and evil. Rest in the Oneness today. Rest in wisdom instead of mere factual knowledge. HALT your strategies and searching. Stop fixing and even "healing." Leave your nets and follow the Instructions of the still small Voice within. Consult the Higher Authority. You are never lost. We know exactly where you are every moment and are right here with you.

Time to build up your TRUST again. Time to stop trying to figure shit out. LISTEN AND TRUST.

23. TRUST THE PROCESS

Essentially, all healing is the release from fear.
- A Course in Miracles

Healing is healing is healing is healing is healing. It is realignment. It makes no difference if it is the healing of a physical dis-ease, or of a relationship, a financial need, a social or political situation or anything else. Each one is the release from fear and the return to inner peace and equanimity.

Release the temptation to continue focusing on the symptom and condition. Gazing mesmerized by the "facts" of the moment will never provide you with healing. Continually turn to the God-in-you to, not talking about the condition, but giving thanks that the process of healing IS happening already. You must shift from terrifying yourself to soothing yourself.

You must not rush this. You cannot watch the clock and the calendar if you want true healing. Keep your eyes focused on the Divine instead. Though the pull of fear may be quite strong, THIS is the time to practice APPRECIATION more than ever. Focus on feeding your spirit and soul with beauty, love, kindness, nature, music and all that makes your heart sing.

This is NOT about doing battle or going to war with conditions. It is not about "getting rid of" anything. What you resist, will tend to persist. Medicines, surgeries, nutritional plans, therapies and body work, etc. must be seen simply as helping to restore balance, not as weapons of destruction. Kindness, gentleness and patience are the ways of true healing.

Say to yourself daily:

God-in-me is guiding my perfect healing now. There is no rush in any of this. It is all happening in Divine Order and timing. I place my future in the hands of God. Every hand that touches me is a healing hand. Wellness is natural for me. There is nothing to fight or attack. I am being gentle and kind with myself. I live in daily gratitude for all the good in my world. I know that God is loving and generous. There is only a stream of well being - there is no stream of sickness, poverty or sorrow. I now release any mental patterns which may have created this condition. I give myself permission to heal. It is safe for me to heal. I have consulted a Higher Authority. There is nothing that cannot be healed. All things are possible for God-in-me. I accept all the gifts of God today and I trust the process of Life. I release all fear and breathe in the peace and Presence of the God

24. THE END

You came forth to live happily ever after.

- Esther Hicks

YOU are the one who determines HOW your story is told, by YOU. You can tell a story of "poor me" or a story of "wonderful, wonderful me." The choice is yours, every day, each moment. But YOU will FEEL the EMOTIONS of the way YOU tell the story. What others are saying or doing is out of your control and ultimately none of your business. Stay in your own yard, beloved Miracle Worker.

When a painful incident is over, let it be over. When a challenge is over, let it be over. Don't keep dragging it into the present, letting it poison the well of this moment. The way is quite simple. You can say, "The End." In this way you are telling yourself and your mind that YOU are ending the story NOW. And you can do this as often as you need to, over and over again until it sinks in and you FEEL it.

And if you want to accelerate the miracle turn-around of energy, you can add, "And I lived happily ever after."

Remember, time itself is an illusion and it is not at all necessarily so that you "need time" to get over something. Miracles are a means of SAVING time so that it can be used more constructively. Why wait a moment longer than necessary?

25. "Thank You" Seals the Deal

Jesus, once more deeply moved, came to the tomb. It was a cave with a stone laid across the entrance. "Take away the stone," he said.

"But, Lord," said Martha, the sister of the dead man, "by this time there is a bad odor, for he has been there four days."

Then Jesus said, "Did I not tell you that if you <u>believe</u>, you will see the glory of God?"

So they took away the stone. Then Jesus looked up and said, "Father, I <u>thank you</u> that you have heard me. I knew that you always hear me, but I said this for the benefit of the people standing here, that they may <u>believe</u> you sent me."

When he had said this, Jesus called in a loud voice, "Lazarus, come out!" The dead man came out, his hands and feet wrapped with strips of linin, and a cloth around his face.

Jesus said to them, "Take off the grave clothes and let him go."
- John 11:38-44

Giving thanks PRECEDES the manifestation because it seals the deal between your conscious mind and the God-in-you Subconscious Mind. Jesus would give thanks and THEN the loaves and fishes would miraculously multiply to feed the thousands. "Thank You" is the sign that you DO ALREADY BELIEVE. You are not wishing or hoping. You only thank when you actually BELIEVE it's already a done deal. Doubt and waffling have been done away with.

Begin today, right now, to move into the state of giving thanks as a way of sealing the deal with God-in-you. Loose the Power that creates worlds through the power of your spoken word. You are often still too timid and wishy-washy because of ridiculous bullshit religious and spiritual brainwashing and fears of being disappointed, let down, or looking foolish to others. You've got to let that shit GO.

Boldly begin to declare things like this:

Thank You God-in-me for my perfect healing.

Thank You God-in-me for bringing harmony and Divine Order to my relationships.

Thank You God-in-me for opening all the right doors for me to walk through.

Thank You God-in-me for showing me the answer to this challenge.

Thank You God-in-me for replacing my anxiety with inner peace and joy.

Thank You God-in-me for dissolving my old mental blocks and releasing me from bondage.

Thank You God-in-me for healing my heartbreak and helping me to move on in Grace.

Thank You God-in-me for bringing forgiveness and restoration to my family.

Thank You God-in-me for my right work and limitless prosperity.

Thank You God-in-me for _____.

26. THE BODY

Miracles praise God through men. They praise God by honoring His creations, affirming their perfection. They heal because they deny body-identification and affirm Soul-identification. By perceiving the spirit, they adjust the levels and see them in proper alignment. This places the spirit at the center, where Souls can communicate directly.
- A Course in Miracles

You must have noticed by now that the entire treatment (prayer) is a recognition of the non-power of the condition (symptom); it deals only with God and is always on the level of God, not on the level of mortal man.
- Joel Goldsmith, The Art of Spiritual Healing

The human problem seems to be one of bodies, bodies, bodies. Everything is seen through the lens of what is happening in the latest serial adventures of the body. These bodies so rarely satisfy the one seemingly dwelling within it - it is too big or small, or it doesn't "feel" right - it hurts, it aches, it won't do this or that, or keeps doing some unwanted thing.

Even relationships are usually seen only through the egoic thought system of what one body is doing with another body, if it is "exclusive," if it is not where you want it to be or with some other body you do not approve of, and on and on and on. Yet through it all, the body is neutral. It is neither good nor bad, so how can it be a problem? Only the MIND is a problem in how it perceives the body. When you are in the ego thought system, you use the body to LIMIT love rather than as a vessel of loving communication and an extension of LOVE.

This fear around bodies is all bullshit. It needs undoing. Miracles UNDO your fucked up thinking about bodies. Isn't that wonderful?

A wonderful metaphysician, Ernest Holmes used to say, *"We believe in anything that works!"* He meant that there is nothing more spiritual about one "remedy" than another. Surgery is not less spiritual than meditation because they are still both merely FORMS. Any actual HEALING is always always always the SAME content - it is the releasing of the body from ALL judgment, guilt, attack thoughts and fear. HOW it is accomplished is between the individual and the Holy Spirit within them on a case-by-case basis. What worked for you two years ago may not work at all now. NOW is your point of power - not then, not later. Now. Go directly to God within. Do not pass go, do not collect $200. Go directly to GOD-in-you.

Cease to identify yourself as a body and all the cultural ego labels of man, woman, gay, straight, old, young, this race or that one, this political party or that one, and all the endless ways you use body identification to further separate from the limitless joy and peace of ONENESS with Source when you are SOUL-IDENTIFIED. Be at peace. Breathe baby, breathe. Make this body your dear friend and not a fearful enemy to be conquered and mastered. Come from love, not fear.

27. No Laws of Scarcity

Darkness is lack of light, as sin is lack of love. It has no unique properties of its own. It is an example of the "scarcity" fallacy, from which only error can proceed. Truth is always abundant. Those who perceive and acknowledge that they have everything have no need for driven behavior of any kind.

— A Course in Miracles

We will be chipping away at you throughout these lessons at your belief in lack, limitation and scarcity. They are illusions and will only bring you fear and suffering. Remember, the vision of one world costs you the vision of the other. You cannot see two worlds at the same time. You will either register a world of darkness, sin and lack - or you will register a world of Light, love and plenty.

Whichever world you choose, your subconscious mind will seek to prove is the right one - and it makes no difference if what it proves is a total lie and illusion. Illusions are as powerful in their effects as the truth, IF YOU BELIEVE THEM. Side with Us in the Laws of Abundance and Plenty. There ARE NO laws of scarcity - only illusions.

Again, this is not about hard work and struggle, for millions work very hard with little or nothing to show for it. This is about alignment, alignment, alignment. It is about BELIEF and KNOWLEDGE. KNOW the Truth, and it will set you FREE. If you believe in limitation and scarcity, there will be endless evidence of it all around you. If you believe you are not enough, conditions will seem to prove it at every turn.

REPENT! Repent means to "turn around" and go in the other direction. When you see limitation, REPENT and go the other way, toward abundance and plenty. There are more than enough opportunities, work, available men, available women, affordable homes, new ideas, places to sit, children, resources, money money money, clients, healers, congenial companions, helpers, avenues for you to give your gift in, people to appreciate your talents, lovely places to eat, good schools, healing modalities, adventures to go on, friendly faces, love love love, romance at any age, and whatever else you can dream up and align with.

The only limits are the ones you allow in. It all starts in positive imagining. Let yourself joyously dream knowing that the Universe has already said, "FUCK YES BABY! You can have that!"

28. Money is Divine Energy

I like money. I believe that it is God's activity, that it is good. I use it with wisdom. I release it with joy. I send it forth without fear, for I know that under a divine law it comes back to me increased and multiplied.

- Raymond Charles Barker

We are going to be encouraging you to get over religious bullshit ideas about wealth, money and success in these lessons. There is nothing unspiritual about liking or even loving money. It is no different than saying, *"I love pizza. I love flowers. I love hummingbirds."* All are made of the same Divine Energy, temporarily taking different forms. It's all God, God, God.

And like everything physical, it can be used wisely or unwisely. It can be used or misused. If you eat pizza until you are sick and throwing up, then that says nothing about pizza. It only means you are using it to meet some imagined need that it cannot meet. It is the same with money, cash, coin, etc. If you are trying to use money to make you feel loved, or worthy, or safe, or anything other than merely enjoying it as a medium of exchange, you are asking for stress.

Nor is it hard to get or have. That is only a belief. Therefore there is no need to hoard it or strive after it. Make friends with money. Invite it like a dear friend you have a wonderful loving relationship with and want to play with. Money responds to your consciousness, your vibration, just like people, animals and everything else does. Money is not playing "hard to get" and you are not being denied it no matter how many mistakes you may have made with it in the past. But you must get over your hang ups about it. You must welcome it and let it in. You must speak lovingly about it. you must believe that it comes when you call it with love. Try using the affirmation by Dr. Barker at the top of this lesson every day to set the vibrational tone for your loving relationship with money and watch how it responds to you in the most delightful fun ways.

29. #DDHD: Dreams Don't Have Deadlines

This is the special means this course is using to save you time. You are not making use of the course if you insist on using means which have served others well, neglecting what was made for <u>you</u>. Save time for me by only this one preparation and practice, doing nothing else. "I need do nothing" is a statement of allegiance, a truly undivided loyalty. Believe it for just one instant, and you will accomplish more than is given to a century of contemplation or of struggle against temptation.

- A Course in Miracles

Time is one of the biggest guns in the egoic thought system arsenal. There is always too little of it or too much, or something you wanted is delayed or happened too soon. And there is the tremendous temptation to think that something is "too late" for you, based on media reports and what others have experienced or achieved. More BULLSHIT! More useless "compare and despair" when you need to be keeping your eyes on your own paper.

When you fall under the spell of this "time" nonsense, you are tempted to begin strategizing and planning and scheming your next move, instead of ALLOWING your JOYOUS connection to Us to open the right way for you in perfect timing and in perfect order. Or you give up in despair and shut yourself off so that you render yourself temporarily inaccessible to the Atonement Principle.

Again, it all boils down to what is almost impossible for humans to do - relax and let go in TRUST that all things are held perfectly in the hands of God within you. We are quite aware of what you need and how to line you up with all the right people and conditions. When there is something to DO, IF you are trusting in

God-in-you, you will do it with great ease and Grace - and usually not even suspecting it will lead you to the fulfillment of some dream or desire. You may have THOUGHT it should happen in your 20's and it happens in your 70's - so what? That is judging according to appearances again.

You THINK you know where you are when you are very lost, and you often think you are lost when you are right on track. Trust Us as the GPS. Throw out your clock and calendar - metaphorically. NOW is your only point of power. TRUST and focus on ENJOYING the journey - you are most likely not where you think you are anyhow. So, just enjoy the view and keep showing up, prepared, on time, doing what you said you would do, with a good attitude. Let Us handle the rest.

30. CAST YOUR CARES

When you have learned how to decide with God, all decisions become as easy and as right as breathing. There is no effort, and you will be led as gently as if you were being carried down a quiet path in summer. Only your own volition seems to make deciding hard. The Holy Spirit will not delay in answering your every question what to do. He knows. And He will tell you, and <u>then do it for you</u>. You who are tired will find this is more restful than sleep. For you can bring your guilt into sleeping, but not into this.
- A Course in Miracles

What to do? What to do? What to do? So many future plans which have not worked out. Now what? Have you learned this lesson in gentleness yet dear Miracle Worker? We know you have already had so many moments in life proven over and over again that when you let go and cast your cares on God-in-you, things unfold in often surprising and wondrous ways. Yet, you still *worry* needlessly about the future, future, future. And sometimes you regret, regret, regret the past. This creates a self-created and self-sustained burden on you that you would do well to question and release back into the nothingness.

When you truly cast your burdens and cares on Spirit, not only does the Answer come, it is done FOR YOU most of the time. Your part is so small in saving yourself from stress and suffering. And yet, you still resist doing just this small part which you CAN do and insist on trying to do the large part which you CANNOT do! What point is there in having a fleet of Angels and then trying to do Their job instead of your own? We see a North Star which is not visible to your limited yes. We know the way to your visions and greater good.

Simply decide that you do not know the way, but Spirit does. Then, set the GPS with your highest intentions and cast the burden of getting there on Source. DO NOT JUDGE the route. Simply follow your joy and inspirations - and take note of your progress. Write it all down as if keeping a lab notebook of test results, because you will quickly forget again and be tempted to try to force your way through instead of relaxing your way in with Grace and ease.

Take a moment now to relax your mind, clear it by giving over every care and concern to the Source within. What burden or worry, not matter how seemingly big or small, is weighing on you now? Give it to Us. We go you Boo. Breathe it out, and know you've made the right decision in giving it over to the Power that holds galaxies in place and keeps the planets spinning in perfect proximity to one another.

31. YOU ARE LOVED BEYOND BELIEF

You who have tried to throw yourself away and valued God so little, hear me speak for Him and for yourself. You cannot understand how much your father loves you for there is no parallel in your experience of the world to help you understand it. There is nothing on earth with which it can compare, and nothing you have ever felt apart from Him resembles it ever so faintly.

- A Course in Miracles

How can We ever explain the unfathomable? You may think you know, but you have no idea. Even those of you who are mothers and believe you have experienced what you think is the most profound and real love in the Universe have not even touched the outer edges of the true love that Source has for you. NOTHING you have ever felt comes close - nothing. This Divine Love is so luminous that it sparkles and radiates even when you are in the deepest depths of despair. NOTHING you do can dim the love of your Source. No "sin" or error has ever had the slightest effect on it. It is truly beyond all conditions. Therefore, it is beyond your understanding.

So, perhaps the best you can do is merely to ACCEPT it as SO. Without necessarily feeling it, accepting it as true can go quite a way in making you available to the miracle of each moment for there is nothing that this Divine Love cannot accomplish. In all your searching for love, it has perhaps never occurred to you that it is already here RIGHT NOW and has NOTHING to do with what "kind" of a person you are. It is not based on your evaluation of your "worthiness." YOU have tried to "throw yourself away" at times because of feelings of inadequacy and separation. But feelings are not facts. They are just feelings. They are not good or bad, true or false. They just are. Try to go beyond the feelings to the TRUTH.

For the next few days, and even beyond, spend some time breathing in and accepting the Truth that you may not necessarily feel by saying to yourself:

I am loved.

I am important.

My life matters.

I matter.

My Source adores me.

I need do nothing to deserve the love of Source.

I am never alone.

I value myself.

I value my life.

I am enough.

I am worthy.

I am loved by my Source.

There is nothing to go in search of.

32. Keep Going in the Right Direction

If you say, *"I am beholding God-in-me as my answer,"* that word goes forth to make the answer appear. If you want the answer, you have to behold the answer. You have to be aware of the answer. You have to speak the answer. When you do this, the answer will unfold.
- Frederick Eikerenkoetter, "Reverend Ike"

Every problem and challenge has an Answer. The Answer is the same to every single one of them - union and Oneness with God-in-you. You may lose faith in your human strengths and capabilities all the time, but never lose faith in God-in-you. It is this Presence that goes forth before you, making straight the crooked places. It is going before you today, right now, to the extent that you are activating it through the power of your intention and YOUR SPOKEN WORD. We cannot emphasize this enough.

There is vibratory POWER in words. Words are containers for power which is either directed for you or against you, BY YOUR OWN DOING. Be very careful of "venting" with those around you because every word you speak is creating your life. Venting is adding meaning and a story to the facts. It is the danger of what you say after, "I am . . . " when you would do much better to simply say, "I am FEELING . . . ". Attaching meaning to the facts is often your mistake. When you say, "My body has this illness and it means . . . " you are usually wrong and limiting yourself. Stating the facts of a disease, a financial problem, a relationship issues is not venting - it is simply sharing information and is fine. It is suppressing and hiding it in fear that makes it fester. And it is fearfully sharing while negatively interpreting and making a disturbing story around it that is problematic "venting" and actually only increases the problem instead of the Answer. You can share the facts and your FEELINGS safely if you are not identifying yourself with the problem and are continuing to affirm that God-in-you has GOT THIS. There is no shame or spiritual "failure" in having problems and challenges. But don't let them get you turned around and going in the wrong direction.

You still may be focusing too much of your attention on the issue and problem instead of on the MIRACLE you want to CREATE. This is much simpler than you may realize. You create by INVOKING. To invoke is to summon, to call forth, to invite. Call forth from God-in-you, the Light that heals and prospers and restores. Be gentle but firm in this and you will have great progress. Do not FORCE yourself if you are not ready, but at least affirm that you are in the process of becoming ready.

There is no race involved. Trust the timing as you keep taking those penguin steps in the right direction until the day when you will actually be able to lift up with wings of eagles and soar! Get used to sharing miracles more than problems. Make a habit of taking note of every sign We send that We are here with you now. Get used to tuning in to Us and to beating the drum of every single crumb of validation that you are loved and guided instead of blowing up problems into catastrophes. You are doing extremely well. Admit it. Look how far you've come instead of magnifying how far you think you have to go. Savor your NOW. Appreciate this moment, this day. It's a good one.

33. YOU ARE PERFECTLY FINE

There is no emptiness in you. Because of your likeness to your Creator you are creative. No child of God can lose this ability because it is inherent in what he is, but he can use it inappropriately by projecting. The inappropriate use of extension, or projection, occurs when you believe that some emptiness or lack exists in you, and that you can fill it with your own ideas of truth.

— A Course in Miracles

You are not shattered, not broken, not wounded, not incomplete or insufficient, and there is no emptiness inside of you no matter what you seem to have lost. And only an unhealed healer would try to take advantage of you by telling you otherwise. Their own insanity compels them to teach insanity to others in the name of "spirituality" when it is utter fucking bullshit. Head for the nearest exit as soon as possible if a healer or teacher is trying to "put you back together" in some way.

Again, We are not saying that you may not FEEL broken or shattered or empty, but feelings often having nothing whatsoever to do with Truth. When you realign yourself with Truth, the feelings will get in alignment with Reality. As a woman thinketh, so is she. If you are SAYING you are empty, you are AFFIRMING IT and CREATING an amplification of that FEELING.

Nothing has ever left a hole in your heart. That is a feeling that poets and song writers have used to describe a feeling which has nothing to do with Reality. It is sentimental drama meant to make you suffer in a "beautiful" way. It is simply an illusion in a stanza. Truth is so much more lyrical and beautiful, but you live in a world in which artists prefer darkness as do most all humans. In fact, only the least talented and cheapest of artists fall on the crutch of amplifying heartache and darkness because they know it sells like hot cakes to ignorant people who know no better. Truth is a 5 star restaurant meal being offered in a world that prefers drive through fast food crap. It's savory going in and then fucks you up when it hits your system, making you lethargic and bloated with cheap emotions. Truth requires a refinement of your palate so that it can appreciate what is truly nourishing and delicious after a lifetime of ingesting garbage.

YOU ARE A CREATOR, not a helpless victim of your emotions. THERE IS NOTHING NOTHING NOTHING WRONG WITH YOU. You were created to be YOU - stop trying to change what was created with Divine perfection. You are not a project to be fixed and worked on. You are a precious gift to be honored and savored. It is only the arrogance of the ego which tells you there is something about you which needs "fixing" in some way. You soul knows you as a perfect spiritual being.

Affirm:
I am filled with the Light of Christ Consciousness. There is nothing missing in me. There is no empty place in me - nothing that needs to be filled. I am a powerful creator, not a victim of loss or circumstances. I can change my mind and change my direction. I do not need to be fixed for there is nothing wrong with me just as I am and just as I am not. God does not create junk. I am not broken or damaged. I am whole, complete, batteries included, ready to go!

34. Invoking Divine Love

Divine Love, expressing through me, now draws to me all that is needed to make me happy and to make my life complete.
- Catherine Ponder

You are not shattered, not broken, not wounded, not incomplete or insufficient, and there is no emptiness inside of you no matter what you seem to have lost. And only an unhealed healer would try to take advantage of you by telling you otherwise. Their own insanity compels them to teach insanity to others in the name of "spirituality" when it is utter fucking bullshit. Head for the nearest exit as soon as possible if a healer or teacher is trying to "put you back together" in some way.

This is Brother Jacob's favorite Catherine Ponder affirmation, but it is only a jumping off point for working with the ENERGY of Divine Love in your life! Remember that miracles are merely expressions of Divine Love. They are Divine Love expressed and in action here on the physical plane. You may want to spend some time working with the above affirmation and watch the miracle working power of it in action - but, you can also simplify it even MORE to whatever best suits your current need or needs in whatever is your own authentic natural voice. We suggest you begin invoking Divine Love at least dozens of times a day, as frequently and naturally as possible.

Here are some ideas.

Divine Love is healing my body.
Divine Love is restoring my health.
Divine Love is guiding my actions.

Brother Jacob

Divine Love is bringing me clarity.
Divine Love is increasing my sales.
Divine Love is healing my heart.
Divine Love is making me rich.
Divine Love is employing me in a fabulous job.
Divine Love is guiding me to the perfect parking place.
Divine Love is my prospering power.
Divine Love is showing me the way.
Divine Love brings me all the ideal people for my staff and team.
Divine Love is opening my mind to wisdom.
Divine Love is filling me with the peace of God.
Divine Love is bringing me great abundance.
Divine Love is protecting my children.
Divine Love is attracting the ideal clients to me.
Divine Love is soothing my emotions.
Divine Love is running my business.
Divine Love is healing my family.
Divine Love is making my house a home.
Divine Love is inspiring me.
Divine Love is helping me find what I need in this store.
Divine Love is bringing wonderful new friends into my life.
Divine Love is helping me forgive.
Divine Love is my success power.
Divine Love is making me attractive.
Divine Love helps me sleep at night.
Divine Love is bringing vitality to my body.
Divine Love is dissolving my resistance.
Divine Love is healing my addictions.
Divine Love is healing my relationships.
Divine Love is drawing my right mate and I together now.
Divine Love is settling the court case with ease and joy.
Divine Love is releasing me from bondage.
My life is run by Divine Love.
I make decisions easily through the grace of Divine Love in me.

And on and on and on. Try it. Your going to LOVE its miracle working powers!

35. Stay In Your Business

These goals, which were important to *him*, kept him on the track. However, once he got the promotion, he ceased to think in terms of what he wanted, but in terms of what others expected of him, or whether he was living up to other's people's goals and standards.
— Maxwell Maltz

Whose business are you in? You must know by now that you can only be happy when you are in your own business. Living up to what you think others want or expect of you is a path to suffering. Living up to the "standards" of your culture or tribe is going to drive you to insanity if you let it.

Instead, live up to the goals and standards of the Source within you if you want the peace and joy that is your Divine Inheritance. Treat others with kindness and respect, and then they'll think or do as they please with that. You cannot control them or control what they think, feel or perceive. The more you focus on THEM, the farther you go from your own center. The Tao teaches, "the farther one goes from herself, the less she knows" and it is true. Stay centered in your Self, and all will be well with you.

Yes, you may not fit in when you do this, but you will also find that much of your anxiety, frustration and depression with dissipate. If people don't get you, they are not your people. That doesn't mean you cannot love them or be in relationship with them, but it should keep you from struggling to GET THEM TO GET YOU OR TO UNDERSTAND YOU. Let it go. That's not your business. That's climbing over the fence into their yard instead of tending your own garden.

When you release others, you release yourself too. You release yourself from suffering. And this allows you to experience the peace and joy of self-acceptance. You are here to manifest YOUR dreams, not the dreams others may have for you. Get still mentally and let this Truth saturate your Being. Relax and let go of what others think. Release the hostages.

Don't get angry at them, get clear in YOU. They have nothing to do with it so release them from YOU wanting them to be different. When you want them to get what they don't get or to approve of what they don't approve of or to see what they don't see, you are in THEIR business in THEIR yard, holding them hostage. Loose them and let them go with love and peace. Then, affirm:

I give myself full permission. I can be who I want to be. I can do what I want to do. I can have what I want to have. I lovingly release others to do the same.

36. YOUR DIVINE DNA

If you want to experience the best of life, you must believe that you DESERVE the very best of life.

- Reverend Ike

You have been equipped and coded to THRIVE in this life. Your Creator did not make you to crawl around like a worm in the dust professing your unworthiness - that is the bullshit of the ego's religions and spirituality. It is over. It is enough. Let it the fuck GO and rise UP!!

No one owes you a thing. No one needs to see your greatness but YOU. And YOU owe yourself EVERYTHING. You owe it to yourself to not ever give up on yourself - to keep on going and believing and loving and expressing more LIFE every day in whatever tiny or large way you can that day. It ALL counts. Simply keep going in the RIGHT direction.

Your human DNA is meaningless because you have DIVINE DNA vibrating through every system, cell and organ of your body, including your BRAIN. But you must NOT beat the drum of limitation, lack, scarcity and fear if you are going to keep your Divine DNA at the forefront of your experience in the physical. INVEST IN YOURSELF each day through your thoughts and actions. Show up for YOU instead of wishing others would show up for you.

Too many of you are priceless unique diamonds lost in a junk drawer of cubic zirconium, and only YOU can lift yourself out of the crap and present yourself to Life as radiant magic jewel seen by appointment only. Don't cheapen yourself any longer. Stop selling yourself short. Shine yourself up and vibrate away all the gunk stuck in the crevices of your consciousness. Start today, right now right where you are. DO something FOR yourself today as a way of showing that you believe you deserve to be who you want to be, to do what you want to do, and to have what you want to have. Do something, no matter how small, to show your subconscious mind that you are taking good care of this precious gem that you are. This will get and keep your Divine DNA humming along so that the better it gets, the better it gets.

37. Joy is Magnetic

Those who attempt to heal without being wholly joyous themselves call forth different kinds of responses at the same time and thus deprive others of the joy of responding whole-heartedly. To be whole-hearted, you <u>must</u> be happy. If fear and love cannot co-exist and if it is impossible to be wholly fearful and remain alive, then the only possible whole state is that of love. <u>There is no difference between love and joy.</u>

- A Course in Miracles

There is nothing more powerfully magnetic and "attractive" in all the multiverses than JOY. When you are in a state of joy, you are being who you really are and are aligned and in what you sometimes call the receptive mode.

But this does not mean that you should say yes to everything that comes when you are feeling joyful. In fact, you should always be very very picky about what you say yes to and what you allow into your vibrational field. Not that there is ever anything to fear, because there isn't, but because you want to be able to maintain your own vibration and say yes ONLY to those people and circumstances which will keep it high and lift it higher. Don't ignore "red flags" - they are part of the sifting and sorting process of contrast. But don't look for them either. Mainly, stay in your OWN YARD no matter what is happening around you and continue to focus on activating more JOY and Divine Love in your days and nights.

YOU are responsible for your joy balloon, so keep it floating and flying HIGH by focusing on the things that bring YOU joy, whatever they are. DO NOT FEEL GUILTY ABOUT THIS.

Humans have the strangest habit of feeling guilty about making themselves feel good. In fact, in your culture you hear a lot about the stigma of depression or mental illness or addiction when nothing could be farther from the truth. Humans LOVE to talk about these things and to "bravely" come out of the closet about them. But when they do, there are COUNTLESS resources for them, meetings and gatherings happening every day all day long, and they are lauded for their bravery and taken in by the tribes. The ACTUAL stigma in the human world is against true joy and happiness. Thriving is something you are supposed to keep to yourself while you turn away from your success and focus on those who are not joyous. This is 100% wrong and is why even though your world improves daily, the humans are more miserable with each passing year. Unhappy people have center stage in the human culture - always. Only humans could come up with an insane concept like, "you are having too much fun!"

YOUR path is different. You are here to activate and radiate JOY with wild abandon! The ONLY way you CAN be of ANY TRUE help to others is by BEING JOYFUL beyond reason. Sacrificing your joy will do NOTHING for others. Instead, continue to progress forward in beating the drum of your own joy, and you will be a beacon and magnet to more joyful experiences and people. You will be a light unto a darkened world, and all while having a ball!

If you want more good in your life, get joyful. It will be irresistibly drawn to you like a moth to a flame.

38. Thank You Divine Love!

Beloved, let us love one another, for love is from God, and whoever loves has been born of God and knows God. Anyone who does not love does not know God, because <u>God is love</u>.

- 1 John 4:7-8

Miracles occur in an atmosphere of belief, faith, and calm receptivity. They cannot be counted on in a vibration of fear and doubt. Gratitude is the extreme opposite of doubt. It affirms that "it is already accomplished." It's a done deal. Additionally, SINCERE gratitude creates a state of alignment in you. As you well know by now, alignment is the name of the game.

You are also aware that miracles are expressions of love - Divine Love moving through you. If you want to accelerate your joyful expansion of miracles, begin to think of "God" as Divine Love. This moves away from the illusory myth of a dude or mother in the sky pulling puppet strings, and brings you in alignment with the Reality that God IS Divine Love. Divine Love is impersonal because It plays no favorites at all. It is that Infinite Stream of well being which flows into wherever there is an opening. Gratitude creates the opening because it puts you in a state of alignment with your desire. Gratitude means you DO BELIEVE!

We are suggesting that you begin to work with this in a very practical daily way now. It could not be more simple, it is simply a matter of living in an almost perpetual state of "Thank You Divine Love for _____." Do this all day long as much as you possibly can. You will find yourself practically getting "high" on the euphoria of an elixir of gratitude and Divine Love. Additionally, it puts you in the vibration of already having, which IS the state of MANIFESTATION. Gratitude as if you already HAVE speeds manifestation 100 times or more.

Make NO distinction between big or small, or in "how long" you think it may take, keeping in mind there is no order of difficulty for Divine Love. Apply the Principle equally in all situations:

Thank You Divine Love for making my dreams come true.
Thank You Divine Love for guiding me to the right sales rack.
Thank You Divine Love for this glorious rainy day.
Thank You Divine Love for bumping me up to first class.
Thank You Divine Love for healing my puppy.
Thank You Divine Love for paying off my debt.
Thank You Divine Love for this beautiful home I live in.
Thank You Divine Love for restoring my marriage.
Thank You Divine Love for the peace in my heart.

39. DIVINE LOVE, JOY AND GRACE

The Soul is in a state of grace forever. Man's reality is <u>only</u> his Soul. Therefore, man is in a state of grace forever.

- A Course in Miracles

We use love, joy and grace interchangeably because they exist on the same frequency. They are your NATURAL state of BEing. They are the extreme opposite of the world of stress that you may have mistakenly thought was your environment. YOUR environment must be the Kingdom within if you are to achieve realization of Who you are and the fulfillment of your greatest good. This is where the state of grace exists and is where your Soul abides.

Therefore, you have a choice today and every day, and in each and every moment. Will you exist in your natural environment of Grace, or within the illusion of stressful time and space happenings? Today could be a day of joyous effortless accomplishment if you will consult the Higher Authority rather than your "to do" list. If you will hourly take even one moment to STOP and remember the Kingdom within you, and allow it to DO the work FOR and through you, miracles will follow miracles. Choose this. It's easier and more fun. Plus, magic. Don't forget, magic.

What YOU think needs to be done today may be totally wrong. You have no idea what really needs to be done today in order for you to experience the miracles that We keep lining up for you. As always, simply ASK for Guidance as you go within - where to go, what to do, what to say, and to whom. Then, forget it and get on with doing whatever is in front of you. No rush. No worry. No stress.

Greater is the Source within you, than that which is in the world. This stuff isn't hard. It's just hard to accept for a mind "hell-bent" on MAKING SHIT HAPPEN. That is not the way of miracles or magic. Get the fuck out of the way, beloved. Good stuff is coming through.

40. Permission Slip

You don't live the life you deserve. You live the life you <u>think</u> you deserve.

- Brother Jacob

Much of this book is about YOU giving YOURSELF permission to be who YOU want to be, to have what YOU want to have, and to do what YOU want to do. This is all about the way YOU talk TO yourself ABOUT yourself - what you believe is possible for you, what you believe is okay for you. THIS is where the inner work comes in very strongly and most importantly. It is remembering that "it's okay, it's okay, it's okay" for you to live the life you choose.

As long as you are in integrity and are not hurting another or yourself, you are good to go. There is no scroll that is going to drop down from the sky giving you permission to please yourself and to make yourself happy. And it is no one's job but your own. No one is coming to save you and no one else is in charge of your happiness. It's all on you, and it is very possible. In fact, happiness is part of your natural state of being, and it usually just needs to be uncovered from the layers of bullshit that the worldly culture has piled on top of it - whether it is religious, spiritual or cultural garbage about putting yourself dead last and being "selfless" or denying your desires or any other ego crap they try to shove down your throat in the name of the ego's religions. This is why miracles are primarily an UNDOING.

Nothing and no one is stopping you but a story in your own head. YOU can end that story by saying "the end" and starting a new happy story RIGHT NOW, without knowing how any of it will happen. How is not your part unless you've already received inspired Guidance from within on the first steps to take. You are on a need-to-know basis most of the time so that you won't rush ahead and fuck shit up. Stay present. Stay in a mode of SAVORING your NOW, while visioning your life continually expanding in all that is good. It is your Divine Destiny and Inheritance.

No, there is no scroll coming down from a mythical paradise in the sky. But in the Kingdom within you can write yourself a permission slip right this minute. It could be something as simple as this:

I, _____, now give myself permission to live the life I choose. I have my full permission to be who I want to be, to do what I want to do and to have what I want to have. I am safe.

41. In the Hands of Love

God holds your future as He holds your past and present. They are one to Him, and so they should be one to you . . . you are but asked to let the future go, and place it in God's Hands. And you will see by your experience that you have laid the past and the present in His Hands as well, because the past will punish you no more, and future dread will now be meaningless.

- A Course in Miracles

We told you a while ago to cancel your future and delete your past, and though it brought many of you tremendous peace and joy, We also know your tendency to keep picking them up again to gradually begin the self-torture. We know you don't mean to, and so We gently bring you back around to your highlighted route of PEACE NOW.

Worry is the mind-set most frequently used when many of you think about your future, even when you are excited about what's to come. You "worry" that something could go wrong or you'll make a mistake or someone else will or that blah, blah, blah. It is a gross misuse of the Divine Creative Power within you, so count on Us to repeat this lesson throughout so that you can once again release yourself into present peace, joy and faith.

We will also keep reminding you that God IS Divine Love. To say you place the future in the Hands of God, is the same thing as saying you place the future in the Hands of Infinite Love and Limitless Miracles. Doesn't that sound better than you trying to figure everything out, cover your ass and spend sleepless nights strategizing and regretting? You can cast your cares on Divine Love and LET GO. Do it now please. Take a nice deep cleansing breath and just let the fuck go as you place the past, present and future in the Hands of Limitless Miraculous Perfect Love. All is well and the better it gets, the better it gets. Prepare for more good than you've ever experienced before when YOU get out of the way and let your mind REST. Believe Us, what you are ready for, is ready for you!

42. Fuck Enlightenment

God holds your future as He holds your past and present. They are one to Him, and so they should be one to you . . . you are but asked to let the future go, and place it in God's Hands. And you will see by your experience that you have laid the past and the present in His Hands as well, because the past will punish you no more, and future dread will now be meaningless.

- A Course in Miracles

This is yet another one of those "spiritual" concepts which is pure bullshit no matter what form it takes. It is a way of building in a false hierarchy in which some are "enlightened" and out of their high state they will "enlighten" the ignorant and "less than." It is taking the ego concept of competition and "spiritualizing" it into another kind of "winners and losers" mindfuck. Reject it entirely and you will find your peace and joy.

What were once the old abuses of religion have easily and quickly found their way into "spirituality" and the self-help/growth movements. On your TV you will see your famous ones having 'soul" conversations with those who turn out to be alleged sexual predators, moguls turned meditation teachers who may be rapists, yoga gurus and "spiritual" teachers who drug and actually brand their sex slaves, not to mention the thieves, rageaholics, narcissists and some inadvertent murderers. How is it done? It is simple. People are extremely gullible when they believe there is something they lack but need - like "enlightenment." And if you add to that crap to buy and "levels" of the structure, you are practically guaranteed a full house of those lining up to be bamboozled and taken advantage of for profit and power.

There is nothing to "get" - nothing to figure out, fix or change. Just relax and open your inner eye to the Light that is already in you. Call off the search. Relax. Relax. Relax. Nothing is missing in you and there is not great esoteric knowledge that you lack. God here, God now. Divine Love here and now. God-in-you, the only Reality you need accept.

All you need really do is continue to gently support yourself in remembering this every day. The books, recordings, affirmations, prayers, crystals, music, and so on, are all here to gently REMIND you Who you ARE and where the Presence IS already. This is all ritual is - a reminder. It's extremely important, but it is not the thing itself. A map is not the territory. And yes, you need daily almost constant reminding with these maps because you live in such a noisy insane world. But this shit isn't hard and there are no levels and no secret knowledge to discover. Let simplicity untwist your mind so that you can see the Light is already here. Open your eyes to the radiance within you. It's all here, now.

Better to focus you attention on simply loving Source and your neighbor as yourself. That should keep you busy enough to forget about bullshit meaningless concepts like "enlightenment."

43. ALIGN SOFTLY

And if you find resistance strong and dedication weak, <u>you are not ready</u>. Do not fight yourself. But think about the kind of day you want and tell yourself there is a way in which this very day can happen just like that. Then try again to have the day you want.
- A Course in Miracles

We know this seems very foreign to many of you because you are so used to believing that harsh interventions and FORCING things is the way to MOTIVATE and CONTROL yourself. But you also know that even when this works, it seldom if ever lasts. Our way, YOUR way, is quite different and is all about gentleness, kindness and patience with yourself. There is no cruelty in this path. In fact, it is all about the dissolving and elimination of cruelty. This is not about FIGHTING yourself - not at all.

You may want to read the Course quote above frequently to really let is sink in. When it says, "you are not ready" it means <u>at this moment</u>. It doesn't mean you won't be ready in half an hour, or next week. But it is saying that at this moment, starting a war with yourself is NOT the answer. When you find that your resistance to love, joy, peace or taking a positive action is high - STOP. Calm your mind. LET GO. BREATHE. Do NOT push harder or you may very easily hurt something.

Instead, ASK for Guidance and help as you release the NEED to DO anything at this exact moment. Go within. Don't just suppress and go into hopelessness - seek ALIGNMENT again with the experiences of peace, joy and love you want. They are ALWAYS possible and available - ALWAYS. Breath deeply and simply imagine again how you want to FEEL instead of what you want to have happen. We are right here. We can only Help by your invitation. WE NEVER FORCE. Relax, and at your slightest invitation, We will intercede on your behalf. Believe it.

44. Awkward

The world you seem to live in is not home to you. And somewhere in your mind you know that this is true. A memory of home keeps haunting you, as if there were a place that called you to return . . . you feel an alien here, from somewhere unknown.
                                    - A Course in Miracles

We call the Kingdom of Heaven within you Opposite World because it is 180 degrees away from the way things are on planet Earth. Almost everything you have ever been taught, even in your spirituality is exactly upside down and inside out. And this can cause you to feel quite awkward at times as you go around bumping into the insanity of the way things are done on the planet.

Inside, you know that things are supposed to go well for you, that you are lovable and others are lovable, that judging by appearances is insane, that prosperity and health are natural, that joy is what matters most. that attack and defensiveness are toxic, and that nothing is more important than that you feel good. And yet everything the world hypnotism teaches is the extreme opposite of these Truths. This can leave you feeling like an alien when you are being your most natural self. It can be . . . awkward trying to fit in with the others who are also pretending to believe in scarcity and sickness and death and finite resources.

Trying to cover over these feelings of awkwardness by developing a false persona will only make you more miserable. Awkward and weird is the wheelhouse of the Urban Mystic. Fitting in is for sponges, not for the Children of Divine Love. Your freak flag is meant to fly sky high so that the others can find you. They need to see you. You owe them nothing except to be Who you truly ARE already.

Home is not a place you go when the body dies. It is right here, right now, inside you. Stop trying to make things happen or make things work. LET them work by cleaning up your vibration and expecting miracles and magic to light your way. YOU ARE A ROCK STAR OF WEIRDOS. Have fun with it. Relax and let go of trying to seem like you belong here or know what you are doing. Just go downstream with your thoughts and enjoy the ride whether you know what you are "doing" or not. Do for the JOY of doing. Be for the JOY of being. Have for the JOY of having. Everything else is just more bullshit.

45. TRUE BEAUTY

Look upon all the trinkets made to hang upon the body or to cover it or for its use. See all the useless things made for its eyes to see. Think on the many offerings made for its pleasure and remember all these were made to make seem lovely what you hate. Would you employ this hated thing to draw your brother to you and to attract his body's eyes? Learn you but offer him a crown of thorns, not recognizing it for what it is and trying to justify your own interpretation of its value by his acceptance . . . Gifts are not made through bodies if they be truly given and received. For bodies can neither offer nor accept; hold out nor take. Only the mind can value, and only the mind decides on what it would receive and give.

- A Course in Miracles

The economy of your culture would collapse almost overnight if humans were to simply give up all hatred and fear of the body. Nations would fall because almost every political, religious and commerce is built upon preoccupation with bodies and their perceived "needs." This is the REAL war on your planet - the war with the body. Nothing is more feared nor hated at some level than the body.

Yet through it all, the body is completely innocent. It is the thing acted UPON by the mind. It is only effect, not cause at all. It is attacked mostly through endless comparison. Remember, the ego literally lives through comparison. Whether it is bodily comparison to a cultural ideal or to how it used to be when it was "younger" or before it got sick or injured makes no difference because it all brings various degrees of suffering and fear.

But this is nothing more than a developed habit. Yes, some of it is the old "reptilian" part of the brain that is in seemingly permanent survival mode but that is just another excuse really. You CAN change this habit to one of simple gentleness and kindness. Release the body from all the ridiculous goals you have given it to "attract" or get you what you want and much of your fear and resistance will dissolve and the body will cease to torment you even if it does not fit YOUR pictures.

Beauty and ugly, well and sick, rich and poor are just STORIES in MIND. They are the ever-changing rise and fall, rise and fall, rise and fall of the physical. Ultimately the only thing that's really true right now, is beloved eternal spiritual being reading the Crabby Angels Chronicles. Everything else is just a story in mind that is either peaceful or stressful. YOU are NOT a body. YOU are free! True beauty is not of the body, it is of the mind. This is the radical Truth that not only beauty but EVERYTHING is in the eye of the beholder.

46. Present Perfect – Future Fabulous

The past is over. It can touch me not.

– A Course in Miracles

Your inner being never looks back.

– Esther Hicks/Abraham

All of your power is in the present moment. Looking back has no value unless you are joyously remembering the love given and the love received as a launching pad for more good to come. There is nothing else back there of any value whatsoever. Period.

<u>You are not what happened to you</u>. Only the ego's dominant belief system of victim consciousness would tell you otherwise. Your inner being knows that the labels that the culture puts on you are still only limits on love and miracles. You are not a label. You are not a tribe member. You are something so huge that no words can encompass your grandeur and limitlessness. Where you came from and who did or didn't raise you is completely irrelevant. You are your own unique creation. The road behind you is covered in mist and you cannot ever see it clearly because of the nature of perception. Stop looking back. ALL your good is ahead of you now, and since you an eternal Being, that is a LOT of good!

Trying to figure shit out from the past is the ego's favorite way of keeping you from living in the JOY and peace and prosperity and goodness of your NOW. Second to that is worrying about the future. It is all foolishness. NOW is your point of power. NOW is your life. Your future is created by what you think NOW. <u>Your life is determined by what you are saying to yourself about yourself and what you believe is possible for you.</u>

It makes NO difference how big a mess you may find yourself in at the moment or whose fault it was or how you got to this point. What matters is what you will make of it through your thinking

NOW. The miracle knows no difference between $1 and $10,000,000, no difference between a headache and cancer, no difference between age 21 and 91. Only YOU can limit the miracle. Instead of limiting, say:

I open myself to this wonderful new day. I do not know what is going to happen and so I allow Divine Love to guide me and to unfold all things in perfect order and timing. Today, I remember to praise and acknowledge the people in my life with words and actions. I am a grateful Creator today and I am creating from my most loving prosperous thoughts. I am a miracle worker and an abundant being of limitless resources. I am a healer and a visionary. Divine activity fills my day and runs my life. I open my heart to give and receive love. I open myself to miracles and love of this wonderful new day. I am worthy. I am enough.
I am worthy. I am enough.

47. Penguins, Eagles and Sailors

Today I will judge nothing that occurs.

— A Course in Miracles

Sometimes you're an eagle, and sometimes you're a penguin. It's all good. Not every day is the same or calls for the same response from you. Don't get locked into one way of being, doing or having. Stay flexible mentally so that you can be centered and SENSE within what the energies are in this moment. Count on the Power and Presence Within more than on any particular philosophy. Some days the sea is calm and it's all smooth sailing, and other days there are storms a brewing, and other times you simply stay below deck and repair your nets. And you may have all three in one day. Do your best to be present on a need-to-know basis as you maintain your inner Connection to Self.

Honestly, most days tend to be penguin days where you will simply be showing up and patiently putting one foot in front of the other, steadily covering ground, but nothing big or exciting happening. This is why you must learn to appreciate the view even though it may not change much day to day. You are tempted to think it should be going faster, that you could be doing it differently, that something is wrong because this cannot possibly be IT. Calm your ass down. All is well. Savor instead of struggling. Clear your mind and do positive aspects of your NOW.

And there are also those exciting times of soaring as an eagle with lovely new views and vistas to appreciate. It's not better, it's just different. Try to remember this. Enjoy it and SAVOR it without trying to make it last or to keep it going. THAT is actually what ruins it - thinking it is going by too fast and starting to think in terms of limitation and finite resources. Clinging to the good suffocates and ends it. Relax inwardly as much as possible even during this exciting exhilarating phase. They are ALL phases. To everything there is a season.

What We are trying to remind you is to stop judging your path so much - to stop judging yourself and your unique ways and days. Stop comparing. If it seems everyone else has dozens of friends and a million things to do, and you have just your cat and no plans this week, so what? There is no "right" way to be, do or have. Or if you are overwhelmed with the needs of others and would just like everyone to go away and leave you be but they are your kids and live with you, adjust your sails baby. This too shall pass.

Release and dissolve the idea that there are times of bondage and times of freedom. Instead, do your best to appreciate and find the positive aspects of the NOW without judging it. This is the path to peace and joy. YOUR part is to program the GPS, not to design the route or try to control the weather.

48. I Am Choosing Life Abundant!

I am the gate. If anyone enters through Me, he will be saved . . . The thief comes only to steal, kill and destroy. I have come that they may have life, and have it more abundantly.

- John 10:10

And God said unto Moses, I AM THAT I AM: and he said, Thus shalt thou say unto the children of Israel, I AM hath sent me unto you.

- Exodus 3:14

If you are trusting in your own strength, you have every reason to be apprehensive, anxious, and fearful.

- A Course in Miracles

Please do keep in mind that the Hebrew and Christian bibles are not history books, nor transcripts of conversations. They are maps of the psychology and psyche of mind. If taken literally, you have seen that they cause war, strife and chaos on your planet. But if you can see them as esoteric lessons where the Truth is behind the actual stories, you can set yourself FREE. Every single story is about YOU and some aspect of consciousness.

Teacher Jesus was not talking about Jesus the person, but rather the I AM within ALL. He said that the ego thought system which dominates your world is a thief of joy and its only intent is to kill and destroy. But the I AM within YOU comes to bring you life more ABUNDANT! The I AM is the Source of Abundant Life! Get in agreement baby! You do not need to be leaning on your own puny human strength, but instead acknowledge the I AM within you and the I AM will direct all your paths

This is why you are frequently reminded "fear not, be not afraid." You are never walking into any place or situation alone, for the I AM has sent you and goes with you - guiding, guarding, protecting, and doing it all JOYOUSLY and PEACEFULLY. If you will stop leaning on people, places, conditions, jobs, institutions, and anything outside of you, and instead lean on the I AM within, all will be well with you. This is why Our affirmations so often begin with "I am . . . " This is to remind your psyche that the I AM is being invoked and will do the doing THROUGH you and not by you.

The ego thought system is always about activating your self-doubt. The I AM is always about activating your courage, confidence, faith, peace, joy and LIFE abundant. Whose council will you allow today? You have but two choices, choose life. Say:

I AM open to receive the gifts of the Universe today. I AM aligned with the joyous Divine Plan for my prosperous abundant good and I know that wherever I go, love flows. I AM walking through the open doors to my good today and I AM closing and walking past all the wrong ones. I AM a center of Divine Love and therefore I AM attracting to me all that is for my highest and best good today. I AM choosing Life more abundant!

49. You Are Worthy!

Your worth is *not* established by your teaching or your learning. Your worth was established by God. As long as you dispute this, *everything* you do will be fearful . . . Once again - *nothing* you do or think or wish or make is necessary to establish your worth. This point is not debatable except in delusions.

- A Course in Miracles

This is <u>not</u> a book of fillers and spiritual desserts. This is not milk for baby mystics needing to be bottle fed. This is meat for full-grown ass Light Workers! This is why We will continue to drive home how vitally important each very simple lesson is. And perhaps nothing it more important or simple than today's lesson. You ARE worthy. You ARE enough. Period. No debate. Sorry.

And one of the greatest wastes of time of the humans has been going into the past to try to discover where and when the feeling of unworthiness came. NOTHING COULD MATTER LESS or be more of a waste of your time and energy. Nothing. It is a useless meaningless journey which DELAYS the miracle of NOW. It also makes no difference exactly how this sense of unworthiness manifests in your life in particular. ALL that need be done is to change the mental pattern to worthiness.

You are worthy. You are beautiful. You are enough. You deserve to live abundantly. That's all there is to it. Say this to yourself like a soothing mantra day and night over and over and over until it crowds out every thought unlike it. This is NOT in comparison with anyone else. You are not better, not worse. ALL are inherently endlessly worthy. It has NOTHING to do with what you produce, offer or achieve. NOTHING. Expect this lesson to be repeated in various ways throughout our daily lessons.

When Master Jesus healed people, he never asked them to jump through a single hoop, did not look to see if they were saints or sinners, did not ask them if they were even sorry for their errors. He never told them they got themselves into this mess to begin with - never even asked them if they "figured out their lesson yet" - He simply affirmed their worthiness by returning them to their natural state of perfection. He REFUSED to even allow the apostles to discuss what the person's errors may have been. They were IRRELEVANT. AND THEY ARE IRRELEVANT TODAY TOO in terms of your worthiness, value and accessibility to a miracle in this very moment. What is asked is WILLINGNESS and BELIEF. *"Do you want this? Do you believe?"* That's the cost of the ticket to get on the Miracle Ride. Only YOU can buy the ticket.

Say:

I am worthy. I am enough. I want this. I deserve this. I believe.

50. Light is Your Power

Light and joy and peace abide in me . . . Why would you not be overjoyed to be assured that all the evil that you think you did was never done, that all your "sins" are nothing, that you are as pure and holy as you were created, and that light and joy and peace abide in you?

- A Course in Miracles

"Enlightenment" is yet another one of those "spiritual" concepts which is pure bullshit no matter what form it takes. It is a way of building in a false hierarchy in which some are "enlightened" and out of their high state they will "enlighten" the ignorant and "less than." It is taking the ego concept of competition and "spiritualizing" it into another kind of "winners and losers" mindfuck. Reject it entirely and you will find your peace and joy.

Light and joy and peace abide in YOU – right now. THAT is what you must activate and REMEMBER no matter the circumstances past, present, or yet to come. The ridiculousness of defensiveness would be funny if it were not so tragic. Who sits in a bright room saying, *"Oh remember how very dark it was before we turned on the lights in here? We must prevent that from ever happening again. We must fight and #resist the darkness no matter what it costs us. We must fight, and march, and rally, and create organizations and support groups to STOP this from happening ever again!"*

No, you need not fear the darkness or it coming again because you KNOW where the light switch is. No matter the form of the fear or lack or loss, your Light switch has never been out of reach. You just forgot about it or got confused. The answer is simply to align, align, align again with the Light of Divine Love within you by IMAGINING what it would FEEL like to be in Light again. As you THINK of Light, you INVOKE Light, not to come to you but to come FROM and THROUGH you.

Your power is not in your resume, your achievements, your intelligence, your skills, your defenses, your physical strength, your money or position. Light is your power.
Say to yourself:

Light and joy and peace abide in me even when I am not aware of them. I can summon them and bring them forth by daily reminding myself that they are there. They are my constant companions and so I shall not fear any form of darkness. The Light in me is my strength and protection. There is nothing to fear.
I am turning up my Light today.

51. No More "Poor Me"

Depression comes from a sense of being deprived of something you want and do not have. Remember that you are deprived of nothing except by your own decision, and then decide otherwise.

Beware of the temptation to perceive yourself unfairly treated.
- A Course in Miracles

Miracles happen when you go from "poor me" to "THAT'S FOR ME!"

Telling yourself the sad story of how and why you cannot be, do and have the life you want merely means you have fallen down into the lowest consciousness kingdom again and are living as a victim instead of as a Divine Creator. And this is mostly a matter of mental habit patterns needing to be changed. Again, how simple is salvation! Repent - turn around - reverse the mental pattern 180 degrees and go the other way.

As always, this is about CONTENT and not about form. You may feel depressed and very sorry for yourself because you miss the physical body of someone who has dropped the body and transitioned into non-physical. Or you may miss the body of someone who is not with you anymore and is married to someone else. You cannot get the BODY back, but the content and ESSENCE you CAN have by going from "poor me" to "that's for me!" Beware of how slyly your mind may make some physical "thing" like a body, house, company, etc. the source of your good feelings. You cannot attach to the physical without suffering. The physical is by its very nature, temporary. Whatever appears will eventually disappear.

But the ESSENCE, the content, the FEELING - that you can have for as long as you choose and there simply are no limits on this. And when you go for the ESSENCE and continue to marinate in that no matter what the outer physical picture shows you, a form which is a match to that will naturally come into your experience. But you cannot keep on getting endlessly turned around and going in the wrong direction a million times a day. Stay steady. Stay focused. Stay FEELING GOOD as much as you possibly can. Set your mind and keep it set - on the ESSENCE of what you want. Keep it set on THAT'S FOR ME BABY AND I DESERVE IT!

52. Prosperity, Your Divine Right

Money, you are welcome in my hands, in my pockets, and in my life all the time!
- Reverend Ike

Very little fills the humans with more discomfort, anxiety, fear and rage than the subject of money. And yet, money is entirely innocent and neutral. It just goes where there is an opening, like any other form of energy. It does not hide from anyone, nor prefer anyone. It is so plentiful that it is now literally a vibration that is flying through the air all around you this very minute, being sent and received electronically from phone to phone, and from continent to continent. Did you realize that vast amounts of money are vibrationally flying through you even as you sit here reading right now? There is simply no lack of it, regardless of what your past experiences may have been.

There is absolutely nothing "unspiritual" about money. That is another bullshit theory taught by the ego's religions who would have you believe that money is somehow not in alignment with integrity, love and goodness. That is like saying that a sweater is evil or unspiritual. It's all bullshit and nonsense. Leaving the word money out of your prosperity teachings is like leaving clothing out of your class on fashion. You must start to RELAX around the subject of MONEY so you can make friends with it.

Additionally, when you judge those who have money, you have set up a barrier to having it yourself. Your subconscious mind will not let you have something that you have judged as wrong or bad. It will always seem to fly out the window no matter how much of it comes in, or you will have a very hard time attracting any to begin with. If you do not TRUST YOURSELF with money, or it makes you feel guilty or awkward, you will have an icky relationship with it. Call bullshit and let yourself thrive in abundance!

Wanting money is NO different than wanting a salad for lunch. NO DIFFERENT AT ALL. SAME. Can you say with no hesitance or guilt something like, *"I want ten million dollars."* Not that you do want that amount (fill in any amount that you choose), but can you say it with as much calm, guiltless, joyful certainty as saying that you want salad and will be having one for lunch? It's time to deal with your money myths.

We'll leave it at that for today. We want you to ruminate, chew on, and play with this idea for a while. We'll keep chipping away at this over time. Just keep on working with your FEELINGS around money for now and start inviting it to increase in your hands and in your world.

53. Money is God in Action

I like money. I believe that it is God's activity, that it is good. I use it with wisdom. I release it with joy. I send it forth without fear, for I know that under a divine law it comes back to me increased and multiplied.

- Raymond Charles Barker

God is in everything I see because God is in my mind.
- A Course in Miracles

It's all God, God, God, Love, Love, Love, Life, Life, Life. Money is just another expression of God in action in your world. HOW you use it and what you think about it is everything. You can use it to punish and terrify yourself, or to lift yourself up and bring more JOY to your world. You can use it to shame and judge others, or you can use it to inspire and sow good into the physical. It really is all up to YOU. The ridiculous ideas "spiritual" and religious folks have about money are some of the most putrid smelling bullshit in all the multiverse.

It is simply an exchange of Divine Energy. The more it goes out with joy, the more it comes in with joy. The more it goes out with fear, the slower and more fearfully it returns. You really must learn to PLAY with it and ENJOY the game as much as possible - not recklessly and foolishly, but consciously and wisely.

We are more than happy to help heal your relationship with money if you will ask Us to guide you in your daily Prayer Treatments. Let Us show you how fun it is to play the money game on your planet when you remove the fear and judgments about it. You must be as little children, and begin as children do by imagining.

Imagine money falling from the sky or literally growing on trees that you pick hundred dollar bills from. Imagine a truck backing up to your home and delivering gold bars and stacking them in your cabinets. Imagine being paid very large sums for the work you do by people who LOVE and appreciate your gifts and talents. Imagine checks coming in the mail to you every day and your phone dinging constantly to denote money being deposited into your electronic accounts. Imagine looking at zero balances on all past debts and paying off your homes, cars and whatever else you might have. Imagine giving large donations and gifts to those you love to give to. Imagine the best instead of the worst. STREEEEEEEETCH your money consciousness to accept accept accept the gifts of the Universe.

Imagine money as God in action in your world.

54. FLIP THE SCRIPT

My Self is ruler of the universe. It is impossible that anything should come to me unbidden by myself. Even in this world, it is I who rule my destiny. What happens is what I desire. What does not occur is what I do not want to happen. This must I accept. For thus am I led past this world to my creations, children of my will, in Heaven where my holy Self abides with them and Him Who has created me.

- A Course in Miracles

You are creating your own experiences, whether deliberately or by default. The more you can embrace this Truth, the more you will be one who creates joyously and deliberately each and every day. Contrast helps to guide you along the way as you notice the difference between wanted and unwanted - choosing to let go of unwanted and focus more fully on wanted.

YOU are writing the script, casting the production, directing it, choosing locations and set designs, making the budget and choosing the overall themes and whether it is comedy, horror, tragedy, or drama or whatever. You can therefore recast, reshoot, rewrite to your heart's content all the way through the production. At any time you are free to flip the script because it is YOUR creation.

Therefore, it is really best to write a script that makes YOUR heart sing than in trying to please an imaginary audience in your life. No one is watching. Everyone is busy producing and watching their own show. Your show is for YOU to enjoy. You. You can stop trying to please the peanut gallery. Have FUN with this - there are no ratings and you cannot get cancelled or receive a bad review unless YOU write it yourself and put the words in one of your character's mouths to say.

Take some time to chew on this. IMAGINE the scenes you would like to play today and write them in your Consciousness and maybe even on paper. Then, LET them happen in their own perfect timing and ways. You do not MAKE them happen. You do not force or coerce. Again, it is the playfulness of a child that you must go for in this. The better it feels to imagine it, the better it will feel to live it. Imagination is everything. EVERYTHING has come from the Imagination of Source, and as an extension of the Source, you have the same power to create from Mind. Use it consciously, joyously and wisely today - and tomorrow - and the next day - and so on.

55. The New Earth

"Heaven and earth shall pass away" means that they will not continue to exist as separate states.
- A Course in Miracles

Those of you who have been studying with Us for a while may remember several years ago Brother Jacob talking to you about the 2012 shifting of one world into two. We want you to know this is an ongoing process rather than a once-and-for-all cataclysmic shifting. Just the same, there began a few years leading up to 2012 and ever since, what Jacob calls a "mass exodus" of people from the physical to the non-physical (those who could not or did not want to make the shift while in the body) as well as people just vibrating out of your life if they were of the old world. That old earth is the one of victims and perpetrators. It is the vibration that is most clung to in spite of the toxicity of it. It may also seem like you "lost" a lot of people, or that you just don't seem to see each other anymore for reasons you cannot quite explain. You may not realize you LITERALLY drifted apart - to different vibrational realities, different planets.

Remember that the vision of one world costs you the vision of the other. Those of you who have been cleaning up your vibration and became devoted to the peace, joy and love of the New Earth may be finding that you are just not as disturbed as you once were by the news even though it may seem more horrifying and tragic than you remember in the past. Many of you are wise enough to not watch it at all. At times you may have euphoria for seemingly "no reason." At other times you may feel grief and sorrow over the "loss" of the old world and its ways and people, even though you were not necessarily very peaceful or happy with much of it. That will pass as you become more rooted in the Kingdom, which is what this New Earth IS.

We are here in record numbers with those like you who elected to come here to help reverse the energies which made this shift possible. Those of you reading this are most certainly teachers and ministers of Light who came to assist in ushering this massive vibrational shift, not through hard work and sacrifice, but through controlling your own vibration and thereby demonstrating to others how to vibrate higher and higher. YOUR JOY creates the bridge between worlds. By learning to not let anyone or anything steal your joy, you fulfill your Function as a Teacher of God. Your JOY is what serves the whole.

You MUST be gentle and kind with yourself, while still <u>maintaining absolute vigilance in staying in alignment, alignment, alignment</u>. You cannot afford to ever get sloppy or lazy about your vibration. Maintenance is even more important than arriving at the proper frequency. No one would ever accuse Brother Jacob of being "nice" but he is certainly the kind of Drill Sargent who gets Mystics to a state where We can bounce a quarter off their chakras! He has created a "no bullshit" zone to learn in, but it is not a mean place at all - it is a place of extreme radical gentleness with the self. You just can't bring your story in with you, and the old world folks think that is unreasonable and mean. But it is the ONLY thing that saves souls. The old victim stories cannot exist in the New Earth vibration. This is why you may still be going back and forth between worlds. The two are still very close together and are only very gradually growing farther and farther apart. The more you are of the New Earth, the less you will even register those on the denser frequency of the old world.

When you dip down into the old consciousness, you have chosen the upstream thinking that sucks you into the old world and all its suffering, struggle and sadness. No worries. Just clean it up and get right back in alignment by REMEMBERING the New Earth. FOCUS on the Kingdom, and you're in It soon enough. This is why it is the deepest of spiritual eternal Truths that NOTHING IS MORE IMPORTANT THAN THAT <u>YOU FEEL GOOD.</u> From THAT place, you can begin to CREATE new relationships with those of the New Earth who, like you, choose to feel good as they take responsibility for their own emotional journey. Take your time. Rushing will not work. Working harder at works of the flesh will be fruitless and frustrating. Remember that birds of a feather flock together, and you will find that one day your life has just the right wonderful people in just the right amount. You'll understand the Principle of effortless accomplishment and living by Grace.

56. ABUNDANCE ANGELS

The universal supply expresses through a law of abundance <u>without a secondary law of limitation</u>. You may treat for abundance with an unconscious pattern of limitation. So you do not have results. On the surface you say that you desire plenty of money, but your subconscious pattern is $325 a week. As the subconscious pattern has more power than the temporary conscious mind desire, you demonstrate $325 a week while you could be demonstrating much more. The universe takes you at your valuation. Increase the consciousness of your own valuation in money. As you do more money appears in your experience.
- Raymond Charles Baker

The only limits are the ones in your own imagination, or lack thereof. YOU set your value in the world in all ways. What others think and believe is none of your business. God-in-you is the Source of your Infinite resources and supply. It IS your supply. Nothing is stopping you from increasing in all that is good in your world.

Please do not think that you are somehow on your own with this. We are here to Help you IF you will call on the Abundance Angels. We CANNOT assert Ourselves into your experience for this would violate your free will. YOU must ask us to intervene and assist you in expanding your Consciousness of wealth, prosperity, opportunity and money, money, money.
We find that many of you are still playing too small mentally and are trying to be "rational" and "reasonable" in your expectations and in what YOU think is possible for you given x, y and z. That is YOU limiting your receptivity with a bullshit story you made up and now defend. Rather than asking Us for money or more opportunities, you should ask Us to Help you expand your MONEY AND WEALTH CONSCIOUSNESS. THAT is where the real issue lies.

It will go much easier and faster if you will start to think of all of this as FUN instead of as something desperate and difficult and hopeless. Money usually goes where the FUN is, haven't you noticed? Money is hanging out at the resort, at the banquet, in the palace - not in the ghetto, among the starving, or in the third world. But humans have reversed the reason why. They think money is the CAUSE, but it's the reverse. You think that the resort and party are that way because of money, but actually money came BECAUSE of the JOY of the resort and party. You think that the lack of money has made the ghetto bleak, but the bleakness IS a REJECTION of money. This is why "you will always have the poor with you."

Don't forget, the "rules" of the world are totally wrong in every way. Opposite World will tell you the secrets of manifestation if you will just be willing to TURN AROUND.

If you want to attract anything GOOD, you must get happy FIRST, before it gets there, or it will NOT come at all. Abundance Angels counsel you first to GET JOYFUL and GRATEFUL if you want to seduce money into your life. Circulate it JOYOUSLY and without fear. Money loves to have FUN and to PLAY. It loves to build and grow and create things and wonderful experiences. Joyous money attracts more money. Don't spend, don't give, circulate. When something circulates, it returns to its point of origin - like the blood in your body.

Start to imagine BIGGER money experiences than you have ever had before that are filled with JOY and FUN for you. Don't give a single thought to HOW the money or resources got there, just imagine all the wonderful and FUN things you will do circulating it. Do this every day whenever you have a free moment. We are ENCOURAGING you to daydream at any time when you do not need to have your attention on some important task before you. Take each spare moment to love and appreciate the flowing of money. This is how you invoke it into your world.

57. REAL HELP

You do not need guidance *except* at the mind level . . . You should ask instead for help in the conditions which have brought the fear about. These conditions always entail a willingness to be separate. At that level, you *can* help it. You are much too tolerant of mind wandering, thus passively condoning its miscreations.
- A Course in Miracles

Every correction and bit of Help is at the mind level. Mind IS the condition which CAUSES and CREATES. We touched on those yesterday and want to make a very brief simple clarification and reminder for you to chew on and USE.

EVERY real condition is a mental one. Only the external form makes them *seem* different. They are all the same. There are NO physical conditions, only effects of mind. ONLY the mind needs healing. Only the mind CAN be healed. Anything external or physical is always, always, always an effect, not a cause.

Therefore, do not seek to attract more money, but rather ask that your mind be guided to a greater belief in personal prosperity. Do not seek to attract a lover, but rather ask Us to Help guide your mind to the realization that you are lovable and worth loving and being with. Do not seek to heal your body, but instead ask Us to heal your mind of a belief in sickness and turn it to thoughts of radiant wholeness. Do not let your mind wander to focusing on appearances as if they were the cause rather than an effect.

Understand?

58. Your True Nature

To be able to abide in the is-ness of God is far better than all the teaching or talking in the world. It is not what a person says that does the greater works: it is the quiet, peaceful realization. The first and very simple rule is not to reach out to God for something, to be sure you do not believe you need a God-power, and to realize constantly that your only need is for the realization of God's grace.
- Joel Goldsmith

Have you whipped yourself up into a frenzy of "doing" again? Perhaps not the actual doing, but the thinking about and wondering about the doing, doing, doing. Thinking, thinking, thinking, doing, doing, doing - it's exhausting, isn't it? And so NOT truly helpful. Only the false self is preoccupied in this way.

Your true Nature is God-in-You. Therefore you exist in a state of perpetual Grace and need not preoccupy yourself with endless logistics and running around like Chicken Little trying to keep the sky from caving in on you, or trying to grab more of what you think you want and need. You must stop wearing yourself out with doing and thinking. Spend more time focused on BEING, EVEN as you are in rush hour traffic (especially then actually).

You can even spend less time thinking about Principle if you are allowing the awareness of Presence to dominate your vibration. No matter how busy the body is, you can be resting inwardly in the Presence and in the state of Grace. You can have serenity in the midst of the storm. You can have it in the absence of what you think you want. You can have it anytime you focus on the realization of it. It is magnetic and it is your safety and security in all things.

Let the Presence go before you, making straight the crooked places and opening all the right doors for you. Less hustle and muscle, and more magic and miracles are what you need. But YOU must strengthen your faith by practicing the Presence more and more and more all that time. Practice develops faith. Instead of doing, let it be done THROUGH you by the Grace of the Presence within. How? By relaxing mentally and turning within as often as possible: "of myself I cannot do this, but the Presence within can do it all."

59. Yes, You

Salvation of the world depends on me. Here is the statement that will one day take all arrogance away from every mind. Here is the thought of true humility, which holds no function as your own but that which has been given you. If offers your acceptance of a part assigned to you, without insisting on another role . . . The arrogant must cling to words, afraid to go beyond them to experience what might affront their stance. Yet are the humble free to hear the Voice which tells them what they are, and what to do.
- A Course in Miracles, Lesson 186

Therefore I say unto you, Be not anxious for your life, what ye shall eat, or what ye shall drink; not yet for your body, what ye shall put on. Is not life more than food and body than raiment? Behold the birds of the heaven, that they sow not, neither do they reap, nor gather into barns; and your heavenly Father feedeth them. Are ye not of much more value than they? And which of you by being anxious can add on cubit unto the measure of his life? And why are ye anxious concerning raiment (clothes)? Consider the lilies of the field, how they grow; they toil not, neither do they spin: yet I say unto you, that even Solomon in all his glory was not arrayed like one of these. But if God so clothe the grass of the field, which today is, and tomorrow is cast into the oven, shall he not much more clothe you, O ye of little faith? Be not therefore anxious, saying, What shall we eat? or, What shall we drink? or, Wherewithall shall we be clothed? For after all these things do the Gentiles seek; for your heavenly Father knoweth that ye have need of these things. But seek ye first his kingdom, and his righteousness; and all these things shall be added unto you. Be not therefore anxious for the morrow: for the morrow will be anxious for itself. Sufficient unto the day is the evil thereof.
- Matthew 6:25-34

And he said unto me, "*My grace is sufficient for thee: for My strength is made perfect in weakness.*" Most gladly therefore will I rather glory in my infirmities, that the power of Christ may rest upon me.

- 2 Corinthians 12:9

The Law of Attraction is the primary Law of Source. It is imperative that you know it and be able to work with it. Through your positive thinking, you activate Law in ways that make your life sweeter and more full of joyous manifestations. But there is one thing that supersedes this and ALL laws, and that is Grace.

Your thinking is only going to take you so far no matter how diligently and consistently you work upon it. For some this will be farther than others, and there is no fault or blame in this whatsoever. In particular for those whose thought is particularly negative or limited, you MUST be quite disciplined and NEVER get sloppy or lazy in your thinking EVEN under Grace. HOWEVER, too much focus on thinking, thinking, thinking can exhaust you even more than hard labor in a coal mine because it can make you soul-weary if it is the ONLY path you take. When you can rest from taking thought, you will see how effortlessly your needs are taken care of.

Grace picks up where thinking leaves off. It is the place of deep inner rest in which the mind can finally truly relax and let go. In fact, in order to fulfill your function, you will sooner or later need to turn it all over to Grace if you do not wish to drive yourself insane with micromanaging, trying to control others and trying to change yourself.

Before you elected to come here, you heard the Call and you answered it, or you would not be reading this book. WE KNEW WHAT WE WERE GETTING WHEN WE CALLED YOU! You are EXACTLY what We needed as part of the Plan, so stop trying to "fix" and change and "improve" yourself. Stop comparing yourself with others. Stop comparing your part with the part others are playing or what they are being, doing or having. It is ridiculous. Relax from all the effort and struggle. Relax. Let go. Trust Us. There IS a plan and it revolves around YOU being YOU. You are so thoroughly and ridiculously important - you have NO idea! None. You judge according to appearances too much so you have not allowed yourself to FEEL the grandeur of your part in the Plan every single day. You do not see what We see from the broader perspective and so you belittle yourself and your part.

Have WE asked you to change? Or was that another one of your bright ideas for "helping" Us? If Source wanted you to be different than you are, Source would open the door for it and guide you through it. But there is only one YOU in all of creation. One. You should enjoy your part and play it full out instead of struggling to get a different role. Stop worrying about all the externals and personalities and let Grace speak to you and Guide you today. Listen instead of thinking. Let the mind go still from time to time today at you TUNE IN to the Voice which speaks for God-in-You. It is the way of the miraculous and it is actually the most fun you can have!

60. LOTS CAN HAPPEN TODAY!

I place the future in the hands of God.

— A Course in Miracles

What could you not accept, if you but knew that everything that happens, all events, past, present and to come, are gently planned by One Whose only purpose is your good?

— A Course in Miracles

More rightly said would be, "I place my future in the hands of God-in-me." And it is equally important to remember that the future is just one moment from now. You may THINK you know how this day is going to go or what is going to happen, but really you don't. And this is GOOD, even if it makes some of you uncomfortable because you have a PLAN you think needs to happen a certain way or in certain timing. Very stressful. Not very miraculous either.

There is another wonderful way which is far less regimented and stressful - and it doesn't even mean that you need to abandon your plan for the day. It simply requires releasing the ATTACHMENT to it. What if God-in-you has a much better way and better timing for you to have things go well today? This is not a dude in the sky pulling puppet strings, but is your Inner Being simply following through on your deep desire to FEEL GOOD and to thrive and succeed.

Your part is simple. First go within and quiet your mind, listen for guidance, make the plan together, and then totally release that plan to God-in-you while you show up, prepared, on time, doing what you said you would do, with a good attitude. You have no idea how quickly We can move things forward when you get out of the way and let go of micromanaging, judging and second-guessing everything. Something that seemed a long way off to your human mind could happen TODAY if you will live this day in joyous TRUST and BELIEF in the Presence in YOU.

61. CLEANING HOUSE

The practitioner or leader in our field who has the consciousness and poise and balance should treat herself, not the patient who tries to "use" her. The patient will then change his attitude or he will leave so that there will be in the practitioner's environment only what should be there and which she has the right to have. If the practitioner refuses to accept her own divine birthright, she is foolish.

I make no hesitation in saying we are here to serve the Truth and not to be used by any living soul.

- Ernest Holmes

The branch that bears no fruit will be cut off and wither away. Be glad!

- A Course in Miracles

Beloved Miracle Worker, if you are going to live in peace, joy and prosperity, you will have to regularly be cleaning your vibrational house. There is simply no way for you to live your inheritance if you are allowing yourself to be used, misused, disrespected, dishonored, and taken advantage of in any way. More than that, you are actually HARMING those who you allow to do so by not insisting they step up to their own Divinity. You help BLOCK their prosperity and healing by seeing them as incapable or feeling pity for them. Pity is not love - it is metaphysical malpractice. Help is wonderful. Pity is destructive.

And if <u>you</u> are one who is always looking to see how you can get the most out of something while contributing the bare minimum, then <u>YOU</u> are doing harm to <u>YOURSELF</u> and will never be able to fulfill the promise you've been given by the Universe. Too many humans pay homage to people who don't know them or care if they live or die, while practically ignoring those who are there for them 365 days a year. And this is what has caused the intense loneliness and pain on your planet today. People invest where there is no return, and endlessly withdraw from accounts that have long been overdrawn and empty. There is no point in looking for a return on an investment that was never made to begin with - it is contrary to the laws of the Universe.

Remember, in Truth, this is a cooperative Universe, not a competitive one. Focus your attention on cooperative relationships and not one-sided ones. Do the inner and outer work to rid your life of leeches and fill it with those whose vibration is mutually uplifting and encouraging. Remember what you DESERVE as a Child of God and settle for nothing less. It will take tremendous courage for you to cut off the branch that does not bear fruit and people will do all they can to play on your guilt. BE STRONG and know that YOU are not their Source. Affirm and believe the best for them, but do NOT allow yourself to be pulled back down. You will NOT pull them up, they will pull YOU DOWN. So YOU must decide if you want to go up, or down. Then, affirm and know that where the dead branch was cut off, in due season, there will be lush and beautiful new growth and so much fruit that you will not have room to hold it all!

62. SHHHH, LISTEN

Very often we are inclined to outline just what our demonstration is to be, whereas the wisest course is to take the attitude of receptivity and let the Spirit inform and direct us in the way in which we should go. Then, if we follow that way, we shall find our footsteps prospered from every standpoint and from every angle. It is when we go contrary to the leading of the Spirit that we encounter all manner of human obstacles.
                                            - Joel Goldsmith

We KNOW what We're doing. You don't need to worry or second guess Us, but you DO need to delegate more to Us if you want to live the life of prosperous seemingly effortless good. We are not your mother. You don't have to plead a good case with Us for wanting what you want. We don't ever get sick of hearing from you, though We did hear you clearly the first time. You don't need to keep repeating yourself over and over, but if it makes you feel better to do so and helps you gain clarity, then please know that We are never tired of hearing from you and never tune you out. We LOVE engaging with you as much as possible. We think you are fun and We fucking LOVE you.

HOWEVER, you cannot receive guidance while in the asking mode. There is broadcasting, and receiving. When you are in broadcasting mode, you are not in receiving mode. They are two entirely different frequencies. Both are necessary, but you cannot really do them simultaneously anymore than you can have a satisfying conversation with someone while you are both talking on top of each other. Speak from your deep within, then shut up and LISTEN. We don't mean you'll hear the Voice necessarily. What We're looking for here is an inner FEELING of release that lets you know that We are on the Field and it's handled on the Invisible Realm now. The physical manifestations will follow.

Please do not try to micromanage Us. You do not see what We do through Our broader perspective. What YOU think of as a shortcut We may know to be the long long long ass way around the bottom of the mountain. Miracles are a means of saving time, remember? *The what* is your part - *how* is Ours. Keep this in mind this week as much as possible. Don't worry, delegate. Then, rest your mind and tune in as a receiver of the signal of Source. We'll get you wherever you need to be for your greatest good. Relax and breathe, relax and breathe.

63. Delegating Miracles

<u>There is one mind common to all individual men</u>. Every man is an inlet to the same and to all of the same . . . Who hath access to this universal mind is a party to all that is or can be done, for this is the only and sovereign agent.

- Ralph Waldo Emerson

It's all already there. There is no need to call in the Light, or the Presence, or healing energy or anything else. What is omnipresent needs only to be recognized and realized in this very moment. Every need is met in the NOW as you align with the Answer rather than the problem. What is known anywhere in the multiverse can be known by you NOW because all is present in the One Mind common to all.

Therefore there is no reason for you to struggle for answers. Go within and relax in the Eternal Presence until you feel the gentle "click" of release. We want to keep these lessons as simple as possible, otherwise We know you will start to MAKE it complicated. In fact, the simpler, the better. It does not matter how complex the problem seems to be or how many other people are involved in the situation or how unwilling they may be - the miracle is created by whoever is saner in the moment.

It is as simple as saying within, *"I don't know what to do. I don't know the Answer. I know the Answer is in this One Mind in which I live and move and have my being so I delegate and release it now to be worked out for me instead of by me. I let it go as I now RELAX into the grace and peace of God. Thanks God-in-Me. I'm on a need-to-know basis - tuned in, tapped in and not interfering."*

64. MIRACLE PLAYER

Miracles are habits and should be involuntary. They should not be under conscious control. Consciously selected miracles can be misguided.

- A Course in Miracles

Very little feels as good to you as knowing that you have been truly helpful to another. It is a huge part of why you came to the planet to begin with so it only makes sense that it FEEEEEELS good to be a miracle worker. Now, a warning :). It is NOT good for YOU to get at all attached to the how, when or who. In fact, very often the ones you MOST want to help are the ones who will never receive it from you. They will take it from a stranger on the street before they'll ever accept it from you. You gotta let that shit go or it will drive you nutty.

And it might also be difficult for you to understand how LITTLE effort is usually involved in creating miracles. They can be extremely powerful even when they are something as simple as a warm smile, or letting someone in front of you in traffic, or in deciding not to have the last word in a discussion - saying congratulations to someone who you assume hears it all the time but who actually never hears it, remembering to put the toilet seat down, not taking the cheap shot, being kind instead of clever and snarky, letting a political comment you disagree with slide by rather than "correcting" the "ignorant," and oh so many more seemingly "small" things. There are NO small miracles. They are all cumulative and they all help to make the planetary shift from fear to love. None are ever wasted - not one drop, even if it

APPEARS that it has had no effect. Judge NOT according to YOUR evaluation please.

LET it be done THROUGH you and not BY you or you will exhaust yourself as another depleted caretaker! In fact, it might help if you stop thinking of yourself as a miracle worker and think of yourself as a miracle PLAYER! Or a miracle vessel, or a miracle artisan, or some other such thing. Make it LIGHT AND FUN, not serious and significant. This way, you can knock out 20 miracles before lunch and not even know they happened. You'll just keep feeling more light and joyous, because that is the result of creating miracles! Miracles should never be serious drudgery or self-sacrifice. The more TRUE miracles you create, the MORE energy you will have, not less.

It's best to begin in the morning by simply aligning with your miraculous function. It can be as simple, easy breezy as this:

"Ok God-in-Me, here I am. Make joyful use of me today. You know how to find me and how to best do it. I assume You're in control here. I'm on a need-to-know basis. Thanks!"

65. BELIEF CHECK

When he had gone indoors, the blind men came to him, and he asked them, "Do you believe that I am able to do this?"
"Yes, Lord," they replied.
Then, he touched their eyes and said, "According to your faith let it be done to you"; and their sight was restored. Jesus warned them sternly, "See that no one knows about this."
- Matthew 9:29-30

"You either believe this shit or you don't" as Brother Jacob likes to say from time to time. Therefore, it is good to check frequently where your belief and faith is residing. Whatever is happening in your life, do you BELIEVE that God can heal it entirely, even instantaneously and totally effortlessly? Is that the kind of faith and belief you have about EVERYTHING?

We are not chastising you in the least, but are merely asking the question for you to ponder and chew on yourself - without blame or guilt. Perhaps about a situation or condition that you have had for decades - whether physical, emotional, financial, in career or close relationships, or anything else? This is not to make you feel uncomfortable or like you are a "spiritual failure" either. It is merely a soft gentle question. Not every healing is the ceasing of a physical condition anyhow. This is not really a question about healing of conditions - it is a question about faith and childlike belief in the Presence within you and what It is capable of.

By the way, healing is not a "getting rid of" anything anyhow - not even a getting rid of blindness as is the case in our quote today. True healing is always of the consciousness, regardless of whether the symptom remains or not. It is a return to PEACE and sanity. It is an end to suffering and conflict.

There reason Brother Jesus told the men who were healed to not tell anyone what had happened to heal them is because he knew that the humans would doubt them, perhaps mock them, and thereby decrease their own faith and leave them blind or worse in the future. There is no sickness worse than losing your faith. Better to be physically blind with faith and belief, than to have working eyes that see only dreary endless limiting "facts" in a world filled with endless miracles waiting to be born through you. That is a soul sickness which the human world is dying from.

SO, very gently now, do you BELIEVE the Presence in you can heal ANYTHING in YOUR life - even this very day? Even instantly? Would it freak you out if TODAY you had a total instantaneous healing that changed your whole world overnight, or would it just make perfect sense to you?

66. PILES OF PROSPERITY

You must sell yourself on money as a spiritual idea until it becomes an automatic subconscious pattern with you. You will find that the people who have the greatest freedom in money are the people who no longer have to think about money. They have arrived at a subconscious conviction that they will always have it. And, they do have money, because they are subjectively convinced of the fact. The people, who have trouble in regard money, have not yet convinced themselves that they can live in this world and have the freedom and use of money. I do not mean millions of dollars; I mean enough to live more than comfortably.

- Raymond Charles Barker

Remember, there is never anyone to convince but your own subconscious mind. You are never selling to anyone but to yourself. You are not convincing a reluctant deity in the clouds, or your worried parents, or your judgmental friends, or your political group or community. The permission you need to thrive is YOURS. The faith, belief, approval and encouragement that you really NEED is YOUR OWN. And once you have that, you will naturally be drawn together with those who agree with your evaluation of yourself. That is all that is ever happening. Like attracts like. Birds of a feather flock together. What you think about yourself will be reflected in those you are drawn to, whether positive or negative.

Piles of prosperity simply means plenty - plenty of money, plenty of love, plenty of whatever companionship you want, plenty of time to enjoy life, plenty of health to do what you want to do, plenty of the goodness and sweetness of life! SEE and FEEL it piling up around you energetically, naturally, normally and with ease. Don't think of these things as something you need to get or attract, but rather that they are all naturally FLOWING into your world as you watch with calm delight and expectancy.

Whatever you want, the Universe can deliver the <u>essence</u> of it to you so swiftly and easily that it can seem like it appeared out of "nowhere" when in fact it's been waiting right there for quite a while for you to shift your energy to a place where you could SEE and RECOGNIZE it. So call off the search and stop all the strategizing and fixing and struggling to figure shit out. Just remember the only limits are the ones YOU align with, then decide to align with limitless piles of prosperity instead.

I am aligned with a limitless Source Which arranges time and space in order to line me up with piles of prosperity in all that is for my ever-expanding good today!

67. ACTIVE PEACE, THEN STEP ASIDE

And that is all. Add more, and you will merely take away the little that is asked . . . Do not assume His function for Him. Give Him but what He asks, that you may learn how little is your part, and how great is His. It is this that makes the holy instant so easy and natural. <u>You *make* it difficult, because you insist there must be more that you need do</u>. You find it difficult to accept that you need give so little, to receive so much. And <u>it is very hard for you to realize it is not personally insulting that your contribution and the Holy Spirit's are so extremely disproportionate</u>. You are still convinced that your understanding is a powerful contribution to truth, and makes it what it is. Yet we have emphasized that <u>you need understand nothing</u>. Salvation is easy just *because* it asks nothing you cannot give right now.

- A Course in Miracles

Are We starting to get through to you with this now? At all? Little bit maybe? It is the most important thing We have to teach you, it is the easiest and simplest, and the most easily forgotten and most strongly resisted.

The more you can RELAX and get the fuck out of the way, the better everything will be. And when We say relax, We mean MENTALLY RELAX. It has nothing to do with laying on a hammock on a tropical island because you can be VERY BUSY mentally, worrying even in paradise. We are talking about a relaxation that can happen even while you are performing brain surgery. It is a calm stillness within which comes from cooperation with a Principle and Presence which is the Doer through you, not by you. Your helpfulness does not come from YOUR good planning and organizational skills! It comes from your

WILLINGNESS to step aside and be joyously used by Divine Love.

You are meant to live a charmed life. You are meant to thrive without struggle or sacrifice. You are a Divine Being, not a limited human creature dragging your ass across the planet. There is a fabulous Divine Plan for you which is about your HAPPINESS NOW, not later. This requires the one thing most do not want to give up - the illusion of control. If only you could realize how stressful and horrifying that illusion is you would be thrilled to let it go forever. But even that is not asked of you. All that is asked is that you can let it go in THIS moment. Forget about tomorrow and the next moment. Just relinquish it in THIS moment and let your mind be STILL as you remind yourself that We are orchestrating and organizing your good beyond what you could do even if you owned the world and every person on the planet adored you, bowed down before you and was working only to make you happy and content.

We know what We're doing, but it never interferes in the slightest with your free will. We do not fight you. We are here to Help, not to do battle or force anything on you. Remember, you are not even asked to understand how this works or happens or what anything means. Lean not on your own understanding of things or you will fuck shit up very badly. Instead, lean on the Everlasting Arms as you just focus on aligning with Grace and the joyous peace of God.

That is all. Go about you day. We'll harass you more about it again tomorrow, and in an hour, and next week, and so on.

68. It's Now, Now, Now

Your emotions are NOW. The way you feel is NOW. Your life is NOW. It's not later at retirement or when the lover gets here or when you've moved into the new house or get the better job. It's now. It will always be now. Direct your thoughts to improve your NOW moments, and the manifestations will take care of themselves.

- Esther Hicks

If We can get you out of the future and out of the past, We will have really assisted you in fulfilling your fabulous Function as the JOYOUS Light of the world! We would love to remove the word "legacy" from the human vocabulary because the way it is thought of is total bullshit. Your ONLY legacy is the love-joy given and the love-joy received while you walk this world. Period.

You could win every award in the world, have your name on monuments and on "star" walks, have libraries named after you, save a nation, grant hundreds of scholarships and fund a revolution, and ten years after your body dies most everyone alive will say, "who?" You could ask a large amount of people on the street to name the presidents on Mount Rushmore and many of them would say, "what's that?" In fact, in one generation, even your own family may not have any memories of you and you may be nothing more than a name on a genealogy report. The groundbreaking legislation you have passed will be totally undone by another administration. Your boss is likely to forget your amazing contribution to the company by the time the afternoon rolls around. It is simply the nature of the humans so don't take it personally, and Buddha told you this many years ago. Even if you left the world the most amazing gift ever given, it would most likely be bastardized and misrepresented - just ask Brother Jesus about that one! Do whatever you do for the JOY of doing it rather than for the effect you want to have. Give what you give for the JOY and satisfaction of the giving rather than to have it be remembered or even appreciated. JOY-LOVE IS your only legacy.

<u>What matters most is your JOY in the NOW</u>! And YOU are fully in charge of that because it is based on your vibration and focus NOW. Now is the point of power. This is why you feel PEACE when you place the past and future in the hands of Source. In THIS moment is your peace, joy and power. Rest in the moment just as it is, and just as it is not - release resistance to what is and put your focus on whatever good there is to be praised. NOTHING is more important than that you FEEL GOOD NOW. THIS is what creates your future, by the way. Feeling good NOW, creates feeling good later too.

This is why practicing gratitude, appreciation and satisfaction activate your joy, peace and alignment with greater good. If you will simply focus on the positive aspects of your PRESENT moments, you will find that the future takes care of itself quite nicely. So, what's good in your now?

69. Don't Force and Fight, Float Instead

You <u>are</u> prepared. Now you need but to remember you need do nothing. It would be far more profitable now merely to concentrate on this than to consider what you should do. When peace comes at last to those who wrestle with temptation and fight against the giving in to sin, when the light comes at last into the mind given to contemplation, or when the goal is finally reached by anyone, it always comes with just one happy realization, "I need do nothing."
- A Course in Miracles

Humans consider it plain old laziness to just float downstream. They will tell you that floating downstream is what dead fish do, not people who are the movers and shakers who make shit happen! The ego will tell you that if you don't get your ass in gear you will "never amount to anything." But you must remember that this downstream is MENTAL and does not mean that the body may not be quite busy - even all day long within this "do nothing" resting and floating. It does not mean that you are not paying attention to what you are doing. Quite the contrary, it is a real focus at last, because you are not preoccupied mentally with stories, stories, stories. You are PRESENT and as you know, you must be present to win!

It is the understanding that you are not "doing" in order to "get somewhere" but that all your doing has become a walking meditation. It is an end in itself. Therefore, the doing is pleasant and calm instead of resisted, forced or frenzied. It is the relinquishment of living a life of constantly trying to get rid of unwanted and striving after what is wanted. Neither is it a complacency which says that you must "endure" a life of sacrifice, pain and suffering. It is the famous "middle way." In this middle way you are not a hapless victim tossed about by the winds of change or a capricious deity in the sky. You are a CREATOR and you are a chooser, but you are NOT the chooser of HOW. You are not a chooser through your schemes and strategies. Instead, you create through alignment, alignment, alignment.

In this way you become a peaceful creator instead of a harried worried pushy one. You come to see that the same Presence which make the planets revolve around the sun in perfect proximity can handle your daily schedule too and that it is not irresponsible to delegate your visions and dreams to this Presence within you. What the world calls lazy and foolish, the Universe calls wise.

Just tune in every day, and as often as feels good to the Source Frequency. It takes very little on your part and you need not speak in some holy tone of voice. It can be as simple as saying, "Hey God-in-Me, I'm available for any fun assignment You have today which will co-create greater good for all concerned. You know where to find me! Peace, out." Then, watch the miracles unfold as you take any inspired action that comes into your clear happy mind. Life is meant to be fun!

70. Masters and Servants

A DOLLAR is a miraculous thing. It is a man's personal energy reduced to portable form and endowed with powers the man himself does not possess. It can go where he cannot go; speak languages he cannot speak; lift burdens he cannot touch with his fingers; save lives with which he cannot directly deal, so that a man busy all day downtown can at the same time be working in a boys' clubs, hospitals, settlements, childcare centers, all over the city.

- Rev. Dr. Harry Emerson Fosdick

You are not here to be a slave to money - money is meant to be a servant to YOU! Too many humans bow down to money and act as if they must suffer and struggle in order to have it come to them. This is totally false and the exact opposite of how Consciousness operates.

Like everything on the physical plane, you have DOMINION over all that you see except for other human beings (because of free will). But you must calmly and strongly CLAIM that dominion in a manner that shows that you KNOW you have dominion. With money, too many humans are treating it like a dog they got at the pound and then let have run of the house instead of training it by being the master. A dog WANTS a master to serve with love and playful affection. And it might surprise you to find out that money is the same way! Money and wealth want a loving master to serve too! Money seeks out an Alpha to serve and tell it what to do, where to go and what to create. We would like you to start thinking of money like a faithful loving dog!

If you are timid and fearful and hesitant with your dog, you will be living in a nightmarish home run by chaos. The very same thing is true in your house if you are that way with the energy of money. You must not be fearful timid and hesitant around the subject of money. Call money to you and let it come running like a happy puppy jumping in enthusiasm and JOY at the sight of you! Be a kind loving master who pays attention to the loving servant and has FUN with it. We want you to LIGHTEN UP around the topic of money and know that it is as plentiful and in need of a home as the thousands of full animal shelters are overflowing with stray doggies. Give money a good home as you lovingly master it and play with it, letting it "fetch" the most fabulous experiences for you. It's a total win-win!

Affirm: *I am a loving master of money and am calling it to me now in ever increasing sums so that we can play together!*

71. Peace, Peace, Peace

I place the peace of God in your heart and in your hands, to hold and to share. The heart is pure to hold it, and the hands are strong to give it. We cannot lose.

- A Course in Miracles

Peace I leave with you, my peace I give unto you: not as the world giveth, give I unto you. Let not your heart be troubled, neither let it be afraid.

- John 14:27

The peace of God is in you now. There is no path to peace other than to recognize it as right here, right now. It is never lacking - you merely become distracted by other things, often meaningless things. The preoccupation with ultimately meaningless things is how the ego thought system steals your joy and peace.

Quite often it's not the huge things that cost you awareness of the peace within you, but the little irritations and grievances that pop up throughout the day. Then, you hold onto them and carry them around where they attract more of their same vibration. If this is allowed to continue, it will start to cause discomfort in the body, and even pain or dis-ease if it goes on long enough.

Therefore, it's better to cut it off and drop it as soon as possible. The more quickly you notice that you do not feel good, the faster you can hit the reset button and drop all grievances and irritations. It really CAN be quite simple. It's a brief conversation with yourself that can go like this:

"I am not going to let this steal my joy today. I'm not going to let this take my peace. I dissolve this irritation and release all hostages. Everyone gets a pass so that I can have the peace of God that is mine."

72. Letting Go, Making Space

I LET GO OF EVERYTHING AND EVERYBODY THAT IS NO LONGER A PART OF THE DIVINE PLAN OF MY LIFE. I NOW EXPAND QUICKLY INTO THE DIVINE PLAN OF MY LIFE, WHERE ALL CONDITIONS ARE PERMANENTLY PERFECT. CHRIST IN ME NOW FREES ME FROM ALL RESENTMENT OR ATTACHMENT TOWARD OR FROM PEOPLE, PLACES, OR THINGS OF THE PAST OR PRESENT. I MANIFEST MY TRUE PLACE WITH THE TRUE PEOPLE AND WITH THE TRUE PROSPERITY NOW.
- Catherine Ponder

You do not ask too much of life, but far too little.
- A Course in Miracles

Almost all growth and expansion is about letting go rather than holding on. There simply is no standing still for any living thing. Even those ancient trees which are seemingly immobile are continually shedding leaves and their old life forms in order to make room for NEW LIFE and more good to express through them. No tree can take on the growth for another. Each one is an individual aspect of the One and must stand on its own. You cannot grow for another. Only YOU can do your growing and you must release everyone else to do the same. This does not mean leaving them behind necessarily but it does mean realizing you are not responsible for another person once they have reached adulthood. You can provide the tools, but you cannot use the tools for them. You can give love, support and encouragement, but not to the detriment of your own joy and peace. This is a world of FREE WILL and each is responsible for walking their own path.

Give yourself permission to live YOUR life and to make YOUR choices and release others to do the same. Stop taking responsibility for the choices others are making or not making in their lives. Get back in your own yard and bless them in theirs, with NON-ATTACHED Divine Love.

There comes a time in many relationships when it is no longer beneficial for the bodies to maintain close proximity. So many students of the Course do not realize that the scribes Helen and Bill did not begin to heal their relationship until they STOPPED "working" on it and Bill moved 3,000 miles away from Helen. She then went into her abandonment story and a descent into "madness" because she refused to DO what the Course had spent decades instructing her to DO. But Bill was never going to be able to change that - ever. Their walk together had to end or he had to join her in the nightmare. In order to LIVE the peace and joy the Course had been instructing them in, Bill had to "separate" his body from closeness to Helen's. In Reality, there is NO separation anywhere in all of Creation.

Your relationships are not meant to be endless struggles and continual compromising of yourself and the desires of your spirit. That is the ego form of loving relationships which is ONLY about bodies. Learn to let go of the FORM. Learn to let go with love. Learn to expect MORE LOVE and kindness and to not settle for less from yourself or others. When you let go of what isn't working, soon the only thing left is what *does* work. Use the affirmation on this page to help you train your consciousness and subconscious mind to stay in the Divine Flow of love and happy expectations of more LIFE.

73. Agreements for Successful Living

Making an agreement with yourself is a quite miraculous and empowering thing to do for yourself. It can radically change your life if you keep it as a kind of North Star to guide you through your days and nights. We have deliberately avoided the word "promise" here because too many humans have negative experiences of that word. Agreement is more the vibration We want to teach here because you know that you can go back and renegotiate an agreement. This is a contract with yourself FOR yourself. It is not another way to beat yourself up for "failing" to meet your goal or intention.

Therefore, We strongly suggest that you work with these agreements, add your own, reword these if you need to in order to make them fit you better, remove any that don't work for you and then sign at the bottom. But what makes them really WORK is if you read them every morning for at least 90 days to get them into your vibration. They will guide you in magical and wonderful ways. At least once a week, read them out loud to yourself. Spoken agreements will fucking rock your world and shift your Consciousness on very deep levels. Some have even framed them so that they were a constant reminder and guide.

- *I take 100% responsibility for my own life, happiness, healing and what I get out of each day and every experience. I do not expect others to fix me or make me happy.*
- *I agree to love myself <u>no matter what</u>!*
- *I agree to do whatever it takes to stay centered and clear.*
- *I take responsibility for communicating my feelings appropriately and I agree to communicate when something is not working for me.*
- *I commit to daily spiritual renewal through conscious contact with God in whatever way works best for me.*

- *I agree to communicate my feelings as best I can without attack or blame.*
- *I do not have to communicate if doing so is unsafe or would harm myself or another person. I seek divine guidance regarding appropriateness.*
- *I will express my love and gratitude to those around me whenever I can.*
- *I agree to ask for help when I need it. I let go of expecting people to read my mind or know what I want and need.*
- *I release my loved ones from my expectations that they will meet those wants and needs once I have communicated them.*
- *I will help others as best I can without taking responsibility for their lives, happiness or experiences.*
- *I release others from participating in my self-destructive patterns and I release myself from participating in the self-destructive patterns of others.*
- *I agree to keep a positive mental attitude and I agree to learn with joy and to trust the process.*
- *I will learn to say no without feeling guilty.*

---

74. WILLINGNESS, WILLINGNESS, WILLINGNESS

Remember that all sense of weakness is associated with the belief you are a body, a belief that is mistaken and deserves no faith. Try to remove your faith from it, if only for a moment. You will be accustomed to keeping faith with the more worthy in you as we go along.

Relax for the rest of the practice period, confident that your efforts, however meager, are fully supported by the strength of God and all His Thoughts.

- A Course in Miracles

We Angels are the messengers of God. Everyone knows this, of course. But in Reality We are simply the Thoughts of God in YOU. Our names and forms and figures are merely illusions within the dream of separation - just as your own body is an illusion within the dream. Some have claimed to have seen Us, just as you claim to be able to see yourself in a mirror. Everything you see is there because you put it there. It's as "real" as it needs to be for you. You all still have far too much faith what you "see" with the body's eyes. But that is not true seeing. True sight is VISION, which cannot be seen with the body's illusory parts.

You try to fill a hole inside you which does not exist. You try to find God, when it is impossible for you to exist outside of God. This is why We ask you to begin to remove your faith in the body in order to increase faith in the Spirit that you ARE. What you yearn for is right here, right now. Always has been, always will be. Do not try to force this - RELAX into it. More and more We are trying to show you that your small and meager WILLINGNESS is all that is asked of you. Source does ALL the rest! Humans have and continue to devise all manner of rituals and practices and works of the flesh to try to reach what is closer than breathing, nearer than hands and feet. You work so HARD to achieve what is essentially effortless. And it often costs you a lot of money as well! People fly across the globe to do what can be done in an easy chair in the middle of a family fight. You merely take a breath, become willing and then surrender to God's Grace. NOW.

It begins with a DECISION, as everything does. Decide that you are now practicing willingness more than anything else. It is the willingness to trust the Oneness even when you do not see or feel it. It is the willingness to listen to Us instead of the voices of the world or of your ego thoughts. I t is the willingness to see with VISION and faith. It is the willingness to stop trying to "fix" yourself and the willingness to see yourself as whole rather than as broken an damaged no matter what you "evidence" of brokenness may be. Willingness. Most powerful practice there is after gratitude.

75. HUSTLING, SELLING, PUSHING & PULLING

Except the Lord build the house, they labor in vain that build it.
- Psalm 127

You cannot imagine the wear, tear, stress and strain you put upon your poor physical and mental bodies by buying into the sales mentality of your culture. Too often you are selling, selling, selling instead of attracting, radiating and magnetizing. This is not how it was meant to be and it is a tremendous burden on your souls. You market, promote and advertise your way into depression, anxiety and insanity. This need not be.

 It's not merely in your businesses that you do this, but even in relationships. The endless changing of the body to make it more "attractive" moves billions of dollars through your economy and makes no one truly happier or more peaceful within. Beyond this there is "charming" people into doing what you want, or "selling" your kids or mates or family on an idea. It is exhausting to work this hard all the time trying to get what you want. Particularly because it does not last and you have to hit the ground running again the next morning to keep all those plates spinning, spinning, spinning. This is what you have INSTEAD of the peace of God which passes all understanding. But there is another, better way.
You can live by attraction rather than by promotion. The way of promotion is the way of never being satisfied no matter how "good" things are. The way of attraction is the way of satisfaction and appreciation as a way of life. It is the way of peace and joy now, now, now. It is the path of trust, faith and belief. It is the path of creative imagination rather than strategizing and manipulating. It is the path of love instead of fear. It is a path which makes NO

sense to the culture and world around you. But then, you have to look closely at that world and culture and ask yourself if it is truly sane and happy.

One way to start to make the shift is by spending just a moment or two in the morning imagining yourself crawling into bed that night, very happily saying to yourself, "Oh, now that was a wonderful day of all the right doors opening at just the right time in the right ways. And it all happened so effortlessly and magically. Thank you. More of that please."

76. Nothing Can Hinder You

Ye did run well; who did hinder you that you should not obey the truth?

— Galatians 5:7

The "who" that hinders is always yourself in disguise. And the truth that is not being obeyed is the truth of being totally who you are, doing what you want to do, and living as you choose to live. Remember that when you make unspoken agreements to play small, to be less, to withhold, to limit your good, it is YOU and not the conditions that have caused your limitations.

The economy or your location is not blocking your wealth, your ex is not keeping you from a new loving relationship, your sick brother is not stopping you from having your own life, the weather is not keeping sales down. Conditions are results, not causes. YOU are bigger than all conditions and you must AGREE that your good cannot be withheld or blocked by anything but a thought or belief.

Your limiting agreements cannot stop the limitless Truth, but they can keep you from receiving and ACCEPTING your own good. Your STORY is what stops you. Change your story, change your reality. The Universe can handle the HOW if you will create the story. No court in the land, no administration, no lack of medical progress, no downsizing, no economic downturn, no genetics, no market trends, no physical "dis-ability" or mental illness, no family history or anything else can hinder or inhibit the good of one who knows who she is and of her Oneness with the

Infinite. Do you agree? You are LIVING whatever you agree with.

You are under no Laws but God's. That does not mean you do not have to pay your taxes or obey traffic laws. It means you are not under the made up "laws" of genetics, world economics, aging, disease, weather and such. Free yourself from the bondage of old agreements that no longer serve you and from beliefs that your good can be withheld from you!

Begin to consciously make happy agreements which serve you in being, doing and having the life you choose. Only YOU can stop you. Only YOU can set yourself free to soar!

77. Healing is Certain

Those who are healed become the instruments of healing. Nor does time elapse between the instant they are healed and all the grace of healing it is given them to give. What is opposed to God does not exist . . . Would you not offer shelter to God's Will? You but invite your Self to be at home, and can this invitation be refused? Ask the inevitable to occur, and you will never fail.
- A Course in Miracles

I am the vine; you are the branches. If you remain in me and I in you, you will bear much fruit; apart from me you can do nothing.
- John 15:5

Early in his healing ministry, your beloved brother Joel Goldsmith was told by Us, *"Man is not the healer"* and it gave him the peace and instruction he needed to get his human self out of the way and allow healing to happen through Grace. You are being given the very same Instruction now. Healing is not from you, but *through* you. And We mean this in all healing of yourself as well. It is not *by* you but *through* you. Please step aside and let the miracle do the work.

Again, your part is willingness rather than amping up your doing, doing, doing. This is just as true when it is a bodily healing as it is when it is a healing of a relationship, a business, a family, a financial situation or a mind. Remember that ALL healing is mental healing anyhow, since all illness is mental illness, no matter the form. It is always the mind which is in need of healing - not the spirit, heart, soul or anything else. Only mind suffers. Only mind needs healing. And when the mind is healed, peace is restored and the outer things are no longer the point of focus.

If you will simply hang on the Vine, which is the Christ Consciousness within you, it is a sign that you are willing to step aside and know that of yourself, you cannot do this, whatever this is. It is a sign that you understand that healing is inevitable and so you have released yourself from worry and warring with conditions. It signifies that you understand that though you cannot do "this" healing, there is a Presence in which you live, move and have your being Which can do all things with great ease.

This does not mean "cling" to the Vine either. That is more of the same human desperation and panic. You must LET GO and know that you cannot be apart from the Vine or you would not even exist at all. This hanging is completely effortless really. The only real effort is in allowing yourself to remember do it instead of hurling yourself into fixing and resisting and strategizing and trying to figure it all out. There is nothing for you to figure out, fix, or change - just an opening to receive the sweet nectar that comes from the Vine into you, the branch. Feast on that golden elixir now and know that you will be guided every step of the way. We will let you know if there is something to do. All the right doors will open and the right people and resources will align in perfect Divine timing and order as you let go and accept that healing is already accomplished the moment you asked. Now, hang on the Vine and let Us love you back to center. Let go of TIME, let go of when, let go of how. Hang on the Vine.

78. Problems Are No Problem

IMAGINING novel solutions to ever more complex problems is far more noble than to run from problems. Life is the continual solution of a continuously synthetic problem.
- Neville Goddard

The Holy Spirit will answer every specific problem as long as you think that problems are specific.

Let me recognize my problems have been solved.
- A Course in Miracles

You must learn the difference between the absolute and the relative, between public relations bullshit and what is actually happening. Too many metaphysicians think if they "do" their spirituality right they will get rid of all their problems with other people, work, money, illness, and everything else having to do with the body. But this is simply a pipe dream they are led to believe by not knowing the difference between when some mystics are teaching from the absolute and applying it to the relative.

It is true that the Path of Light is lit by Grace and miracles and that much of the cheap drama problems dissolve away as you continue to walk it. Life is no longer the roller coaster ride of one horrendous problem after another striking terror into your heart and mind. But you live in a realm of contrast, and that will look like problems to you at some point most days. Master Jesus had many problems - the Pharisees and Scribes attacking him, the apostles not following simple directions, people wanting him to do everything FOR them, and so on. And many famous metaphysicians in your history have simply hid their illnesses, relationship issues and financial problems from their students and the public out of fear of looking bad and losing their ministry. It's bullshit.

Brother Jacob likes to use the word "challenge" because it inspires rather than depresses him, so what you call it is up to you. Ultimately it is simply the contrast of the world of polarity. In knowing what doesn't serve you, you can choose what will. It is a guide to choosing. In the absolute there is no contrast and nothing to choose between because all is LOVE and JOY - and this is what confuses students from time to time. They hear or read something describing the absolute and think it is about the relative. The absolute is where all is ONE and it is the realm of Reality. The relative is the realm of contrast, differences, the physical. The Answer to every problem is to rise up in Consciousness to the absolute where all is One, instead of focusing on "getting rid of" or "fixing" the physical conditions. The condition is nothing to be ashamed of or embarrassed about. You are not a spiritual failure because you are having problems.

The appearance of problems is MEANINGLESS. You create them for various reasons because of what you want to learn from them or what you want to heal. This is actually not that significant. What matters is how you MEET them - whether you choose to learn through pain or through JOY. THIS is how you can gauge your progress - not by the appearance of problems but by how much you are able to maintain your peace and even joy in the midst of them and whether you fall into poor me victim thinking or turn to the Source within to patiently and gently heal your mind. And it is true that it makes no difference if it is your first day on the path or your 50th year - the Principles are the SAME for all and the issues you face will not be all that different from day one than it is on day 5,000. YOU are what changes as you learn to use how you FEEL as your guide remembering that nothing is more important than that you FEEL GOOD whether you have many problems or none today. AND the better you FEEL, the more the problems will begin to dissolve away anyhow. You will realize in time that your problems are so much smaller than they were when you began this journey. But that doesn't mean you still cannot let them ruin your day if you are not vigilant.

79. The Secret

How do you do it? Self-abandonment! That is the secret. You must abandon yourself mentally to your wish fulfilled in your love for that state, and in so doing, live in the new state and no more in the old state. You can't commit yourself to what you do not love, so the secret of self-commission is faith - plus love. Faith is believing what is unbelievable. Commit yourself to the feeling of the wish fulfilled, in faith that this act of self-commission will become a reality. And it must become a reality because imagining CREATES reality.

- Neville Goddard

The secret is no secret at all of course. It is right out there in the open, taught by mystics and metaphysicians for thousands of years. It's just that so few believe it, it seems like some mystical esoteric information. It is disregarded as irresponsible child's play, not to be taken seriously at all by intelligent people.

If there IS any secret in your culture it is that hard work is NOT the answer to prosperity, abundance, health, happiness, loving relationships, a great work life or thriving. Again, not hidden, but notoriously disputed, and argued and defended against - with a vengeance in most cases. Yet all you have to do is look at humankind's history of slavery and know that their backbreaking work did not prosper them in the least, nor bring them any joy. In fact, the main true "religion" of the humans is hard work and suffering. There is a reverence and respect for "hustling" and "making things happen" which is 100% insane and which causes the vast majority of your depression and diseases. It is completely contrary to Truth.

Here and there some are catching on. All you need do is observe how much wealth and success is available for those who PLAY with joyous abandon! For example, observe how many of your sports figures play during a season and then spend the rest of their year mostly doing as they please. And there are those who have become wealthy making videos of themselves playing video games or cooking or even whispering! They were not even sitting around visualizing stacks of money coming in, they were simply using their IMAGINATION to JOYFULLY PLAY TODAY! They did not "outgrow" the use of their IMAGINATION and ability to play and share that joy with others.

Is this starting to sink in at all?

80. Nothing Is Unhealable

Every time you hear that something is "incurable," know that "they" have not yet discovered a cure and you must go within to find your own healing.

- Louise L. Hay

Healing is not a miracle. The Atonement, or the final miracle, is a remedy and any type of healing is a result. The kind of error to which Atonement is applied is irrelevant. All healing is essentially the release from fear.

- A Course in Miracles

The greatest disease of your world is fear. The ego mind therefore loves the concept of "incurable" because it simply allows the state of fear to be prolonged and even justified. Fear kills billions more bodies than any germ, virus or chronic condition. This is why inner peace is the goal of any Course which is teaching miracles and Truth.

Your very best "medicine" is always going to be whatever amplifies peace and diminishes fear. And how can you have peace if you are at war with some condition of the body, or with the body itself? It is a ridiculous concept. In fact, if you can do whatever healing work you are doing and then mostly FORGET about the condition the rest of the time, you would be astonished at how many "incurable" conditions would simply continue to diminish or even disappear entirely. Distraction from problems by putting attention on gratitude and appreciation is not some sweet old religious tripe. Since what you focus on increases, it is WISDOM to focus on Divine Source 10 times more than on any physical condition that is upsetting you. God is always on the Field and there truly is nothing to fear.

It is up to you and your Guide whether you use Western medicine, herbs, bodywork, meditation, yoga, crystals, surgery, psychotherapy, nutrition, life-coaching, medical marijuana, faith healing or a combination of many different things. Everything works because it is all about the healing of the mind, and whatever helps your mind helps everything. In the end, it is the peace that is the healing. The Atonement is the return to inner peace through Oneness with Source.

KNOW that nothing nothing nothing is unhealable. The Mind that created the body can restore it and adjust it and balance it in ways your conscious mind cannot possible do. Relax. It's not about being clever and figuring it out and solving what you think is a bodily "problem" once again. Instead, simply focus on loving what is, whatever is. Let Divine Love be the salve and balm to any illness or dis-ease you may experience. Stop any war you may have with what is happening. Divine Love is the answer, whatever the problem. You are lovable. You are safe. All is well.

81. EXPECTING IS ALIGNING

When your peace is threatened or disturbed in any way, say to yourself:

> I do not know what anything, including this, means. And so I do not know how to respond to it. And I will not use my own past learning as the light to guide me now.
>
> You cannot be your guide to miracles, for it is you who made them necessary. And because you did, the means on which you can depend for miracles has been provided for you. God's Son can make no needs his Father will not meet, if he but turn to Him ever so little.
>
>   - A Course in Miracles

Take a nice deep relaxing breath. Let your shoulders drop as you release any tension in your neck and head. Let your belly go soft as your let all the thoughts begin to slooooooow down for a few moments. Breathe in the peace of God and breathe out tension and stress. Just let go, let go, let go, let go. There is nothing to grab hold of, nothing to get rid of. There is nothing to get, or fix, or change. There is just this gentle opening to receive the Grace already given.

Let go of leaning on your own understanding, but instead acknowledge the Presence of Grace as your guiding force, knowing that all things are held perfectly in the hands of God. Tell your mind, "peace, be still."

Know that there is a Power and a Presence filling and surrounding you in every moment, guiding you and aligning you with your greater good as long as that is what you want and you do not interfere. This is taking a mental vacation from worry and excessive thinking, thinking, thinking. You can do this to the extent that you place the future in the hands of God. Let Divine Love relax you and take over your past, present and future. This is a day of gently unfolding miracles and magical doors opening for you. You can EXPECT things to go well for you today. You can EXPECT the best. Expecting is aligning. Aligning is creating.

82. Creation, Not Competition

You are to become a creator, not a competitor; you are going to get what you want, but in such a way that when you get it every other man will have more than he has now . . . When you rise from the competitive to the creative plane, you can scan your business transactions very strictly, and if you are selling any man anything which does not add more to his life than the thing he gives you in exchange, you can afford to stop it. You do not have to beat anybody in business. And if you are in a business which does beat people, get out of it at once.

- Wallace D. Wattles

This is an insane world, and do not underestimate the extent of its insanity. There is no area of your perception that it has not touched, and your dream (illusion) is sacred to you. That is why God placed the Holy Spirit in you, where you placed the dream.

- A Course in Miracles

True prosperity, abundance and success is never at the expense of your joy, inner peace, health or loving relationships. Competition and HARD work is NOT prosperity or abundance - it is the old ego scarcity principle in disguise. It says that there is only so much to go around, only one can win, and that you have to hustle and grind in order to get what you want. What could be MORE insane? Everything you have learned here is the extreme OPPOSITE of Truth and Reality.

Your world is going entirely in the wrong direction at a faster and faster rate of speed, yet YOU do not have to be heir to that world. You are NOT a victim of the world you see. YOU are a CREATOR not a reactor. AND you do NOT have to "fix" the world or heal its insanity. That is entirely hopeless and a huge part of what keeps people trapped in the nightmare. No, you WAKE UP from the nightmare by first easing into a happier dream. The happy dream is born of practicing satisfaction instead of dissatisfaction. The ego thought system is based on insatiability. The finish line moves along with you so that no matter how much "progress" you make, you are still just as far from where you think you need to be. It is endless hunger and thirst. It is hell.

There is another better way. As you begin to practice gratitude, appreciation, satisfaction and self-love, you shift into a higher dimension of living. You may find that not much changes externally, or maybe it does. You may look the same, dress the same, have the same job, home, friends, but you will NOT be the same. And yes, you do smile more frequently. You become more childlike without being childish. You learn to PLAY more and more. It doesn't mean you are irresponsible and don't keep your agreements or that you do not get your work done. It does mean that you give up the concept of struggling and thinking that work is about bondage and joylessness. In fact, We want to start you out with a new affirmation to shift your paradigm:

The more I PLAY, the more they PAY.

83. LA DOLCE VITA

"We took God as our senior partner, and we asked for guidance in our work. We prayed that we would attract the right men to do the job and that Infinite Intelligence would reveal the perfect plan for the manufacture, sale, and distribution of our products. We attribute our success and achievements to the direction given us by our Higher Self."

Some of these men were builders, architects, engineers, business executives, and directors of mines and other vast holdings. They used God as their guide, advisor, and counselor in all phases of their lives, and they prospered beyond their fondest dreams.

- Joseph Murphy, Your Infinite Power to Be Rich

There is a very sweet Life available to all who will tune OUT the crazy noise of the ego culture of fear, lack and limitation and TUNE IN to the Source's guidance within. You are NOT on your own and you do NOT have to figure everything out. You HAVE ALL the Help you need if you will simply go into partnership with the Infinite on a daily basis.

We are urging more each day, amping it up in fact, for you to recognize how much you need to LET GO of the lies and bullshit you've been taught about struggle, sacrifice and lack. But that is only half the formula. The rest of it is ACCEPTING the Truth in its place. And the Truth is JOYOUS expansion of good for YOU without suffering and bondage. But as you know, you are so free you can even choose bondage. Choose LIFE instead please. Choose ease and fun and downstream thinking.

Make Source your partner and get in alignment with the happy Divine Plan for your good. There is nothing to do to earn or deserve it -it is the gift of Grace. It is yours for the taking. Stop "hustling" and start humming along with the great Mother Tao. The Way of Life is for everything to get better and better and better as you go. You are not meant to decline and contract as you grow. Your best years are still ahead of you when you understand the Law and practice alignment with Source.

For most, it starts with PERMISSION. YOU are the one who must give YOURSELF permission to be who you want to be, do what you want to do and to have what you want to have. You need no other. You might be surprised how many humans have not even given themselves permission to be happy and to enjoy the day because of some fucked up idea about aligning with those who suffer. Remember that the Course tells you "true empathy does not mean to join with another in suffering." The only way to help the suffering is to not be one of them. You cannot give what you do not have. YOUR JOY brings more joy to the world! Let your joy light up the world simply because it is FUN. Life can be so FUN - don't miss out on it.

Yes, you will have tribulation in the world, everyone does. But it need not break you. You can overcome the world by the daily renewing of your mind. Learn to taste the sweetness of life every day. Let us Help you. Partner with Source by inviting Source to run the show FOR you and THROUGH you. You have no idea how many gifts are lined up outside your door right now waiting for your slightest invitation.

84. IMAGINATION HARDENS INTO FACTS

Haven't you observed that at a certain time of the year money is tight? Why? It's a habit; it's a transmitted state. You fix the fact in your mind's eye that money is tight in the month of December, and, if you received fifty thousand today, you will loan the money out or give it away before December goes by, so you will be tight again. It's a peculiar slavery, this thing called nature, in the sameness of forms in transmittted life.

- Neville Goddard

An assumption, though false, if persisted in will harden into fact.
- Anthony Eden

Imagination is more important than knowledge. Knowledge is limited. Imagination encircles the world.
- Albert Einstein

Your world is overrun by facts, but few seem to understand that they are the RESULT of habitual ways of thinking and vibrating. It is done unto you as you vibrate would be a very nice way to put it. If you are going to change something, you will need to change the vibration that is active within you first. FIND A WAY to FEEL GOOD, or at least better if you want the facts to change. FIRST the vibration - the facts follow.

And surely you have seen how your culture manipulates those "facts" all the time to skew toward whatever it is they are trying to sell you in the moment. They INTERPRET the facts in IMAGINATIVE ways in order to produce the result they want. And it works like magic.

For instance, in the quote above, there is a certain vibration that one has about money in the month of December. The

VIBRATION creates the shortage. The VIBRATION creates the HABIT. And vibration is mostly the result of whatever STORY you are telling yourself in regard to that subject. The story creates the vibration which creates the facts. It's a very orderly Universe.

This is why imagination is much more important than facts. You IMAGINE a NEW story in order to CREATE new facts - but you DO it just to FEEL GOOD NOW. You are not doing it in order to manifest or change "things" but rather to change how you FEEL NOW. EVERYTHING is NOW, NOW, NOW. Tell a story in your mind NOW that FEELS GOOD regardless of the "hard facts" of the moment - imagine a happy outcome to all things for you. Imagine happily ever after.

Brother Jacob

ABOUT THE AUTHOR

Jacob Glass is an author, spiritual teacher, mentor and the mad Montecito Mystic. To order his other books, see his live class schedule, watch online videos or receive his weekly class recordings, see his website: jacobglass.com

Made in the USA
Las Vegas, NV
30 July 2025

25584204R20111